INTERROGATING THE ABYSS

CHRIS KELSO

Interrogating the Abyss

ISBN-13: 978-1-954899-01-8
ISBN-10: 1-954899-01-7

Cover design by Mike Corrao

www.apocalypse-party.com

First Edition

Printed in the U.S.A

INTERROGATING THE ABYSS

CONTENTS

INTERROGATING THE ABYSS

Thinking about an introduction. Thinking about how I can properly articulate a 32-year existential struggle with the abyss and how I can condense my findings into an 'introduction.' I suppose there are only refined questions. Like: what happens when we walk home on wind-torn and lonely nights, through the alleyways of our private towns, warmed and drowsy with malt and muted consciousness? We all have our maps. And we know there is a direct route, from the end of the social-night to the beginning of comfort, safety and dreamhood. We escape the pub and foot the pavement from point A to point B. A cocoon of cosy amniotic fluid awaits. On our short journeys, we can reconstruct conversations and events that befell us. We can bask in the new freedom from other people's company and expectation. It is exhilarating to escape our social duty. Or, if you're like me, we can explore new anxieties of the day ahead.

But eventually, we will make it home to safety and comfort—if we stick to the path. If we follow the known route. However, our desire to shed the nights' skin can often leave us apprehensive and agitated, as if we were snakes attempting to shrug off a tight but rapidly wrinkling hide of our own. We are warned that whoever fights monsters should see to it that, in the process, he does not become a monster. Will delaying comfort make you comfortable being a monster yourself?

I am beckoned by the darkness of an alleyway. I approach, brave with whisky and beer, but self-aware enough to consider the existential significance of contact with the abyss. I step over all manner of detritus, over obese sleeping shadows and pillars of my fear. I see the dark heavy shape that summons me. I kneel to it, consider submersion. Then I suddenly remember my inability to swim. I cannot hold my breath. But I'm here now. Will I ever be able to return to comfort? And do I even care...? Some introduction. Probably fitting.

DEMONSTRATION

Morning/Winter
Maybe 8am/maybe earlier.
Light yet to crack
the retina of a cephalopod-ink sky.
When I heard the music of confrontation
and not for the first time.

*

Gagging sound, from outside.
Rusty machine with defective components,
trying to swallow some piece of oversized input.
Hard hack/suffocation procedure
bumps against window.
And another noise
working in dissonance.
Oversized input/being eaten alive.
Chest compressions with trench boot.

*

Sensing muted commotion of frantic resistance.
Muted by the eating machine,
I wonder,
What is it?
Answers lie behind the curtain.
Answer/More a lesson.
Mouth/eyeballs cut dry.
Had to look behind the curtain.
In that moment, I remember seeing all my Barbie's/dollies,
and thinking about how sickeningly childish they were,
and how I would probably never play with them again
after this lesson.
Body arid/embarrassed.
What was I about to learn?
Draw back curtain and I see it: two birds, mid-flight
—a seagull with the panic-cycling legs of a crow dangling from its huge maw.
Birds cannibalising their own.

*

Seagull's eyes rolling back to a hideous perspective,
As if the mass of crow were forcing the physical structure of the seagull to alter, distort.
Like when a python dislocates it's jaw
to eat a farm pig.

*

Wings of the crow/gone.
Only mad legs fight for futile sentience.
And the gull's wings batter against the glass of my bedroom window
as if it wanted me to see this.

*

The crow, now in the final stages of terminal secretions,
willingly engages in pterygoid walk
to lower abdomen.
Two shuddering gulps/gone,
legs an' all.
My naïve lesson:
Greed can eat death,
make as much as you can.
I bury fear behind wealth
until I realise they are the same.
And I pity the gull,
realise the world is a one-dimensional monster
Domnatio ad beastias.

This poem was inspired by a traumatic event from my fiancé's childhood. She was awoken one morning by a violent altercation coming from outside. Choking, screaming. Struggle and squawking. The glass pane of her window was being battered by someone, or something, and it froze her in bed for almost 15 minutes. She summoned enough courage to approach the window and inch back the curtain to reveal a giant slavering seagull eating a crow. I'm assured that this image was as surreal and unsettling as it first sounds. My fiancé watched in abject horror as the monstrous seabird completely consumed the Dark Muse of Poe in two gulps. The gull looked at her, exchanging a smug warning shot, before flying off. My fiancé was utterly traumatised by this incident and she's convinced it ruined her innocent and idealistic attitude towards life. I mean, how could it not? Maybe this is a painted bird scenario—someone daubing a seagull with black paint and releasing it into the sky only for the rest of his flock to reject him. Failing to recognise the blackened seagull, the flock sent their alpha to devour it. My fiancé is convinced there is a lesson in here...

I TRANSGRESS

"Without Contraries there is no progression. Attraction and Repulsion. Reason and Energy, Love and Hate, are necessary to Human existence. From these contraries spring what the religious call Good and Evil. Good is the passive that obeys Reason. Evil is the active springing from Energy."

—William Blake

William Blake makes the point that 'good' is not about living up to a higher moral code, but rather, it's about being passive, weak, and in line with reason—'bad' isn't about doing horrible things to others, it's about expending energy, independence, creativity. The best of us transgress. We should be proud of it. Certainly not ashamed.

It all starts in the beginning of our literary journey—there is a clear didacticism behind almost all popular literature that is assigned (written for children by adults), and often makes a point of quelling the independent curiosity of young people. The possible intention here is to establish a clear separation between childhood and adulthood. Mainstream adults have an inbuilt desire to keep children innocent and any deviation from this is depicted in literature as an immense tragedy. They employ Christianised behaviour techniques like guilt to ensure that their own projected fears about growing up are maintained.

Unsurprisingly, many children's authors hope to turn popular Christian paradigms of defiance and divine punishment into schemes for growth—which seems noble enough, but can be of great detriment to the attitudes of the following generation. They grow up timid, castrated and unfeeling. But what if our young protagonists fuck and suck their way through adolescence and nothing is learned? No one grows. No one reflects on their outrageous behavior. Sex and violence prevail. What if we gave the kids Dennis Cooper instead of Mary Alcott or Dr. Seuss? What if we taught *The Marbled Swarm* or *Fight Club* or *Exquisite Corpse* to young folk ? Some authors believe disobedience is a natural residue of creative expression, others try to enforce punishment for challenging the status quo or portray rule-breaking behaviour as an absolute heroic last resort. But according to people like William Blake, someone without wild urges is not a real or defined organism . There is something vital missing, no matter how imperfect. It is a crucial part of the whole animal. Then we grow up and find an *American Psycho*, or a *Trainspotting*, or a *Querelle of Brest*, and everything changes. This type of fiction encourages the pursuit of knowledge and actively criticises the monolithic, authoritarian aspects of moralistic society. And, honestly, this is what we need to survive the apocalypse. After all, transgressive fiction embodies such fundamental aspects of the human experience.

Among these fundamentals are: initiation and the transition from innocence to experience, the nature of good and evil, the consequences of knowledge, the notion of free will or individual responsibility, and so on. Writers like Samuel Delany acknowledge the need for rebellion and understand that it is indeed natural. Traditionally, the urge of the writer is to first create a solid differentiation between good and bad. Once clearly discerned, the writer can explore the grey in between. But revelling in the darkness is interesting and worthwhile. If you've read Delany's Hogg—a story about a pre-adolescent boy called "cocksucker" who is sold into sexual slavery—you'll know that beauty can be extracted from our darker compulsions. The story focuses on such deviant behavior—coprophilia, coprophagia, molestation, incest, urolagnia, necrophilia—but the writing is ethereal and crisp. There is no grey. Only black transgressive shadows . Given the recent institutional changes in education, family relations, coupled with the rise of corporate conglomerates, most books are driven by commodity, which inevitably dictates the tastes and strictures of fiction. These books aren't bad, but they're usually boring. They appeal to the depleted, part-time animal. But suffering exists across all walks of life. To pretend like it doesn't is deluded and there's something to be said for confronting suffering (even by vicarious means). But literature, like music and all forms of art, will eventually run out of new places to go, so must turn to cannibalisation. If this is the case, then why not cannibalise the parables of suffering? Sodom and Gomorrah, man.

Historically, there is a similarly conservative tradition prevalent among anthologists, even today. There remains a strange resistance to the inclusion of new or risky writing by editors, instead choosing to favour the idealisation of the adult's nostalgic past—or simply continue the ritual of including the old guard of 'great' writers like Alexander Pope, an 'assigned poet' whose work is turgid, dated, and irrelevant. The 'meaner bards' continue to fall by the wayside. It's interesting that old-guard snobs like Ed Lucas, anthologiser of the landmark book of poetry, A Book of Verses for Children, should be so trivialising of his subject matter. This was a common attitude towards fiction as well—work was often chosen based on the 'great' works of our time, regardless of their appropriateness or relevance to real life. Transgressive fiction can be the most edifying and satisfying literature available to a person. A good anthology is a celebration of a fantastic beast and the mystery and potential of humanity. I will try to avoid anything which reinstates daft conservative ideals (for example, the need to supply girls with fear of their own sexuality) and so in a flurry of Rabelaisian defiance, I bring you this! An anthology to appeal to your inner child.

But I transgress... Sodom and fucking Gomorrah, you animals.

COMBAT SHOCK: BUDDY GIOVINAZZO

Opening Scene—

(A still frame of a boy watching TV, the glare illuminating his face)

I used to nourish myself on a strict diet of late-night trash TV…

A loan soldier appears, weaving in and out of the rice fields of Da Nang; an infantry rifle clutched to his chest. My innocent eyes fastened to the screen. My knees were a little numb from leaning on them with my elbows for so long. Parents in bed. The soldier with lank black hair is sweat-slicked, muddy, and terrified—I would soon discover that this was Frankie, our titular hero (or anti-hero). Something about his face hits me in the base of my gut; it's a face I recognise.

Tortured, hopeless, raked of something vital.

Images of Frankie then become interspersed with archival stock footage of the Napalm bombings. The only thing missing is 'Ride of the Valkyries.' It's a pulse-spiking scene, but all I can focus my twelve-year-old gaze on is Frankie's face. I realise that

I recognise his face because it's the same mask of existential helplessness I wore myself, and continue to wear. I've never seen an actor so real, so relatable.

My dad woke up, came into the living room and yelled at me just as Mike the starving junky started to open up a septic abscess in his arm with the end of a coat hanger so he could tap a vein. That was a heavy image. For both of us. I'm convinced that this must've been a watershed moment in our relationship together, that my dad's opinion of me was shaped and fortified hereafter. You see, my dad has always considered me weird and wilfully morbid. He's a great guy and a great father, but he doesn't understand that part of me at all.

It's funny, he actually remembers the whole incident. I think the extreme impact of Mike the junky seared itself onto his mind's eye. So *Combat Shock* even made a cursory impression on my dad, who is a rather robust character from provincial Ayrshire, all calluses and brawn.

Another thing about this movie was that it was so low budget, but my infantile brain got so wrapped up in the sense of dread, I barely even noticed. You should believe me when I tell you that the opening act of Buddy Giovinazzo's *Combat Shock* is as hair-raising as any Vietnam War movie the BFI might recommend. Just ask Gordon Kelso!

Then we're in a rundown Staten Island apartment potted next to an active railroad. Frankie's life is arguably worse now he's out of the VC. The harsh, Kafkaesque jungle of 80's NYC is a different existence entirely. Frankie is unemployable, unskilled and lives a truly bleak reality. His depressed wife nags him every day and the constant rumbling of passing trains is interrupted only by his deformed child, Rikki's, awful yowling—presumably a result of Agent Orange poisoning. Everything has gone wrong. His toilet is broken, the milk is sour, and his Converse are busted. The family is 'living like rats.'

We get a sense that it's all building up to some awful conclusion, something Hubert Selby would've concocted in the delirious heights of his Streptomycin treatment—the whistling kettle and dripping tap are a bass intro to some great impending final chorus of agony. Frankie soon learns he is to be evicted.

There are a number of things that make *Combat Shock* such a standout—not least Giovinazzo's remorseless cynicism. I was the most depressive young man—even before I was a teenager, I was quiet and obsessed with dark things. This movie provided some much-needed perspective.

Ricky Giovinazzo's soundtrack is another notable quality in the movie. In the opening scenes, he musters a score so apocalyptic and epic your heart will thud in your ears. You'll be praying for it all to end, and yet, it feels like Frankie's torture could never end, in this life or the next. This is a stark contrast to the ominous synth, the quiet after the bombs have dropped, measured, deliberate.

Giovinazzo himself describes this film as a cross between *Eraserhead* and *Taxi Driver*, and these are fair comparisons, but before I'd seen either of those movies, *Combat Shock* struck me on a primal level, and in a profound and terrifying way, it helped shape who I would become as an adult. This was darkness that was relatable. I'd never seen anything like it before.

"The terror is real, it's part of me now and I can't escape it..." comes the haunting voiceover foreshadowing war.

What makes *Combat Shock* such a Troma aberration, aside

from its mature tone, subject matter and unyielding straight face throughout, is its subtlety. This might sound strange for a movie produced by Lloyd Kaufmann (and which features a prosthetic baby that looks like a rubber version of Edward Much's *Scream*), but Giovinazzo is an auteur. Take, for example, the directorial nuances he employs.

Combat Shock originally appeared on the festival circuit under the title *American Nightmares*. Of course, the MPAA had objections...

If you read his books or watch any of Giovinazzo's movies, you'll become instantly aware that the worlds and characters he smears across your brain are so utterly void of light or hope, the velveteen darkness feels like the only place to be, the only place of mercy. I can relate to this. This movie demands that its audience accept the film on its own terms. The screaming innocents as deafening as the whistling of a falling Daisy Cutter—you better be ready for the unrelenting conflict that's about to unfurl before your very eyes, because once you've seen it, you cannot un-see it.

I hunted down Buddy Giovinazzo. He sent me his direct number and I called him in Berlin. I was nervous as fuck...

Sorry if I sound nervous, sorry about my accent.

Don't apologise. I got a thick New York accent...

You sound all romantic, like Woody Allen. But thank you for being so kind.

Thank YOU. I'm pretty stoked you guys are so into *Combat Shock* in the UK.

You should definitely come to Glasgow.

We actually came up to Scotland, to Edinburgh and wound up staying for a few days because we liked it so much.

Did you go to the Fringe festival?

No, it was called the FAB, the FabFilm Fest. We just had a great time and were there during the big ash cloud, about six years ago. All the stores were selling gas masks and face covers.

That's pretty cool.

Yeah, I think it was in Iceland or something at the time and was affecting all surrounding countries.

I think we get all the shit from surrounding countries. I think it had something to do with an eruption of a sub-glacial volcano or something.

Yeah, it was crazy.

If you have any intention of coming back over let me know.

I absolutely will. We've just been in LA for three months so we'll be chilling out in Berlin for the next year, but maybe after...

Were you working in LA?

Yeah, I was there for a show. We go, my wife and I, back every year for a few months.

I meant to ask; how did you end up in Berlin? Relocating from New York to Eastern Europe must've been quite a shift?

I was actually living in LA before I came to Berlin, so I initially moved from New York to LA. I was in LA for three years before moving here to Berlin. I pretty much moved here because I couldn't afford to stay where I was. I mean, I wasn't working. After I did my second feature, *No Way Home*, I couldn't get any work for three years. Things were getting worse and worse financially and I was in major fucking debt, so I had a chance to come to Berlin and live for free for a few months and I figured I had to do this because I couldn't stay where I was anymore. So I figured I'd come to Berlin for a few months then go back to LA and restart my career. But once I got to Berlin, I fell in love with the city. I mean, I was completely at home here—even though I didn't speak any German and I didn't know anybody, it was really like New York for me, the New York of my childhood. Then I got a call from a German company who said, 'We hear you're living in Berlin. Why don't you work for us?' It turns out my second feature was actually very successful in Germany. They knew of it. So, I decided to stay. I was happy here. When I realised I could work here, I said, 'Fuck it, I'm gonna stay.' And I did.

I know you've been working on Leipzig Homicide.

Yeah, I basically work on German TV movies that play on Sunday nights. That's how I live, that's how I finance my independent film career.

Is it satisfying creatively, emotionally, spiritually?

It's not as rewarding as writing and directing your own material. I'm basically just a director over here. I do like directing something I didn't write though, it means I get to do something I wouldn't normally do. It's also great for working with actors. You get better and better the more you do.

It's weird because the first time I came across your work it was the novel Potsdamer Platz, which was a sort of filmic novel about organised crime in Berlin (My horrible accent ruins the title of this book. I actually called it Potsdamm Plazz but Buddy sees the funny side). There was a lot of speculation that Tony Scott wanted to turn the book into a big budget movie, what happened with that? I mean, I know Tony Scott has since passed away but...

Yeah.

Was it close to becoming a movie?

Yeah it was fucking close. Tony Scott bought the rights in 2000 and right up until his death kept buying the rights every year. He was always going to direct it but every time it got close he'd be offered a bigger film. One that paid him more money. So we came close, maybe three or four times, to really almost getting it made. It never happened though. He was a great guy and he really loved the book. I would've loved to have had him direct it.

(Pause to close window for hailstorm that has swept through Berlin)

I downloaded this recorder app for my phone and it only records in five-minute increments, which is really annoying. So every five minutes I have to restart the device. So I'm going to have a hell of a time transcribing about 25 separate recordings!

Shit man, that is annoying.

My fault for not being better prepared or having a Dictaphone. So, let's talk about *Combat Shock*, which is a film that really fucked me up as a boy in his mid-teens. The part of Scotland I'm from is pretty hellish. The West of Scotland is tough. I'm originally from a place called Cumnock which recently had the inauspicious accolade of being 'Britain's worst town'—so there's an idea of what kind of place we're dealing with here. My mum and dad were really protective of me growing up, and I didn't get to leave the house very much, so I was pretty sheltered. But I remember *Combat Shock* was on TV, on channel 4. You used to get quite interesting films on channel 4 at night—and it was like 10 minutes before Mike the drug addict is using a coat hanger to open up a septic arm wound. It was absolutely horrifying, and obviously the scene at the end with the baby. It was so relentlessly bleak. It was horrifying

but kind of instantly relatable. I was quite a morbid teenager and have become a fairly morbid adult, so it really appealed to my sensibilities, but still, I think that scene and the scene from Alien where the chestburster erupts from John Hurt's chest are two images that have burned themselves on my psyche. I wasn't very age appropriate to see those things but they really stayed with me and actually informed the way I wrote in my early novels. Then obviously I read, *Life's Hot in Cracktown* and realised you were a master of all forms.

That's how I feel about it too. Have you seen the movie *Life's Hot in Cracktown*?

No, just the book, but I thought it had tremendous literary merit.

Thank you. The DVD's pretty hard to get a hold of. The film takes place all at once, so it's more harrowing than the book. The film is basically five stories out of the book, I had to narrow it down. They take place during the same timeframe. So it cuts from gangs to prostitutes to kids in the hotel, then all comes together in the end. I'll send you a link to the movie, I have a password.

Cool. I imagine the book is quite difficult to film because the book is such a literary experience. There are elements of rap and street poetry, and there's a focus on the prose and how it's written. The film will obviously be much more visceral from an imagery standpoint. I'll buy it when I get paid next, I promise.

I'll hold you to that, sir.

I actually contacted you quite a while ago and I don't think you replied. Or I figured maybe he's too busy, or that's quite an unprofessional way to contact someone.

(Buddy talks to someone out of earshot)

Sorry I'm just talking to my wife, said I'd call her back. She's in Hamburg.

Is your wife German?

Yeah, she is. The only German woman in Germany.

I know that the re-issue of the DVD has a lot of great special features, and the commentary is interesting, but I'm quite poor so it makes sense for me to just call you and ask you yourself. How did you wind up casting your brother Rick in the movie? I understand he's primarily a musician?

My brother is a very shy guy who's never acted before or since. I think we should try and get him to speak about his role. He saw the screen-test on super 8 and he said he was better than all of them. So I cast him. I needed someone for two years because I knew I didn't have the money to do it quickly. He turned out to be perfect. He's really sympathetic. I don't think Mike the junky would've been as sympathetic, I was going to cast that actor the first time. There are four short films I did before *Combat Shock*, and I cast Mike the junky in all of them. He's a film professor in North Carolina and still makes low budget features. He's a good guy.

NOTE:

It's difficult for Giovinazzo to find an American or British publisher because his work is very dark—which I find curious given my own work is wilfully depressing and dark, and I've never struggled to find a distributor, even though my work is inferior to Buddy's in almost every way. He writes his books in English and they're published/translated into German, a method that has worked well for him and continues to work for him.

He tells me about his plans to set up *Potsdamer Platz* as a German/US co-produced six-part miniseries. Netflix and Amazon in Germany are desperately looking for material, and Buddy intends to exploit the market. This will hopefully interest them because it's about American's coming into Berlin.

There are arrangements to shoot in Germany with US actors so it'll still appeal as an international project. Buddy repeatedly expresses disappointment that the book never found a big publisher who could get behind it.

Giovinazzo delivered a true Troma masterpiece—but not just that, a true snapshot of Reagan's America and a deserving entry into the Vietnam War canon. "I go back there every night," Frankie tells us, and our guts churn at the prospect of a human being revisiting such an awful memory during sleep. Giovinazzo's frightening vision almost didn't make it to the screen.

Before it was ever made, one of the gaffers on *Combat Shock* who worked on *Splatter University* with Troma told Buddy to submit

Combat Shock to Troma. In fact, Buddy thought the movie had initially been rejected by Troma (a director with the company said Kauffmann had watched *Combat Shock* and didn't like it). He tried to sell the movie elsewhere for a year and strained to get it in film festivals. Never to be put down without a fight, Giovinazzo called Troma headquarters personally and asked to speak to Kaufmann himself. He asked Lloyd to reconsider the movie. Kaufmann claimed never to have seen the film. A day later he called Giovinazzo back and said he was in love with the movie and that he'd be honoured to put the Troma name on it.

The director who told you the movie hadn't interested Kauffmann sounds like a cunt.

Yeah, he was. I think he was jealous. They re-screened the movie and bought it right away.

How long was it between *Combat Shock* and *No Way Home*?

Combat Shock really hurt me. It wasn't liked by anybody for years. People who watched it thought they were going to see an action movie because posters were advertising it as the next *Rambo*. There's no gang fights or battle footage. I'd be up for jobs and when they asked to see my first feature they'd look at *Combat Shock* and they wouldn't want to work with me. It's not a genre film to them. It's a genre film now.

Is that when you started writing novels, during this hiatus?

Yeah, I started writing novels because I couldn't get any film work. I was frustrated. I knew that any time I wrote a script I needed a ton of money to get it made, so I'd have to find someone to give me money, and I just found that impossible to do. So I started writing books because when they're finished they're finished, and you just a find a publisher. You have much more creative freedom writing a book. So I wrote *Life's Hot in Cracktown*, and I guess I got it published in 1991.

Without kissing your arse, your novels are excellent. You transition from screenwriter to novelist was seamless.

Well, thank you. Screenwriting involves a lot of reading. I remember reading Jim Thompson a lot and after a while, I said I could write a book like this. Jim Thompson's stuff wasn't overly complicated, he was writing about criminals and the underworld. That's a world I love, so I just started writing stuff like that. But, as you said earlier, I could never make a living writing. It'll take me a year or four years to write a book, and you only earn like a few thousand dollars. You can't live on that.

But during the actual production, did you have assistant directors or anyone to kind of guide you? Or were you thrown in the deep end.

I had total 100% control. No one's money, all my own money. Total freedom. I had a film professor, Phil Niblock, who was a great guy and supported me. He'd write me a letter from the college to the police saying to please let me make the movie—even if I got stopped by the police, I could pull out this letter from my university and they'd read and see I was a film student. But I had no one looking at stuff telling me to do this or that. Which was both good and bad. Good because I'd get to make the exact film I wanted to, bad because someone with more experience would've told me to take some stuff out.

So what would you have changed? Can you watch it again and still be happy with it?

I'm proudest of the last thirty minutes. The uncut ending is so harrowing, it's like a trip to hell and I'm really proud of that. If I had to do anything else different, I'd probably make the film shorter. I would've cut out some of the bad acting or worked harder on the acting. I think my brother is so good. I think all the actors are really great.

I realised you had a cameo in it. Were you the guy at the doll office?

Yeah, I just came in for a short hello.

So what kind of difficulties did you face? Was it a tense set? What was the atmosphere? Was it just a kind of giddy excitement because everyone really believed in the project? I imagine it would be pretty terrifying?

Nah, it was fun. It was totally not tense. We didn't have a schedule, there wasn't any money involved, we weren't paying people, and there was no overtime. In that way, it was like making a student movie. Having total and complete freedom to work with your friends, with people you like. Part of the problem is that some of your friends aren't so talented. So there are many mistakes, and you can't complain because you're not paying anyone. But it was exhausting because there's not enough people to do anything. I would do everything. I was production designer, editor, sound editor, cleaning up the set. If you look at the end credits, there are practically no props, no production designer, no production manager or line producer or any of that. We didn't even know what any of that was, so it was really a calm, quiet set. There were days in the jungle where it was just me, my brother and one other guy. We just had like a two-person crew, plus my brother. So it was exhausting, but it wasn't stressful. It wasn't a business to us at all.

I know you did a segment for Theatre of the Bizarre—so when you work now, or even when you worked on *No Way Home* with Tim Roth, was that much more of a professional set-up? Did you have assistant directors at your disposal, or was it still pretty much just you doing everything?

No. *No Way Home* was a real film with a real crew. We had maybe forty people, we had everything that I never had on *Combat Shock*. That was real. I had producers, a production designer, I had a good camera person. So that was a real movie. Despite that, we were still very loose on set. We were able to change things, we were able to improvise. I worked very loose with actors. Something would happen on set and I'd say that's a better idea than what we had planned, so let's shoot that instead. Same thing with Theatre of the

Bizarre. It was really low budget, no one got paid, but it was also a real film and a real crew. We had enough people to do everything we needed to do.

So do you ever think about going back and doing what you did with *Combat Shock*? You getting together with some of your friends and making something for no money?

Well, I did that in 2012. I made a low budget horror film for a hundred thousand dollars called *A Night of Nightmares* that went around some festivals. That, to me, was kind of like doing *Combat Shock*. We had twelve shooting days with a small crew and a small cast. I loved it! The problem is you can't live like that. You wind up doing a film like that, and at the end of the film you lose money, and you still have to pay to live. You have to pay your rent and everything. You're not getting paid enough, but still, if I liked the project and I liked the script, sure I would do that again.

Hey man, I forgot to tell you a story from shooting. The house of Frankie Dunlan, this house we rented downstairs, we shot on the second floor there. We rented it for a month and it was really nice. The landlord painted it so it was fit for a family, you know. My special effects guy, Ralph Cordero, we had to make it looked rundown see. So Ralph said he could put latex on the walls, put ink in the latex and make the walls look dirty and grimy, then at the end of the shoot we could wipe the latex off, kind of like a rubber. It'll peel right off. So we did that, we painted every wall, put up really horrible wallpaper, anything to make it look horrible. Then at the end of the shoot, we started peeling the latex off, but the walls were disgusting and filthy and we didn't realise the ink in the latex had seeped into the wall. So all the walls were fucked. We had to re-paint the entire house.

Shit...

Worse than that, in the bedroom where Frankie kills his wife, we used gallons of blood for that scene. So anyway, we spent like a week cleaning up the blood form the bedroom. So I'm out of the house, I'm cutting the film in the editing suite. A week or two after I left the house, I get a phone call from the landlord, his name was Artie. He was really hysterical. He was showing a family around the house and when he went to show them the bedroom, blood started to seep up out of the wood. I didn't realise that, of course, wood will absorb any liquid. So the floorboards, even though we cleaned it, the blood came up to the surface. So Artie was screaming at me, "What did you do?" So I said to him to relax, it's not blood. It's syrup. And I had to prove to him that it wasn't blood, that we didn't kill anybody and we shot a movie there. We laughed about it afterwards but...

IN CLOSING:

Buddy Giovinazzo feels strongly about his subject matter. He reminds us of the utter pointlessness of war as villages and huts and innocent people are expunged. Frankie, in his sweat-stained boiler suit, continues to wander the streets, bearing witness to a different kind of social decay. Frankie has escaped from one hell only to reawaken in another.

A man betrayed by his own country, who must live in poverty and squalor. The walls are a cascade of graffiti in deluge. The children are prostitutes, and the most deprived extremity is usually set as default. The greyness is mesmerising also. Of course, Giovinazzo's sense of place is impressive. Even a dog with a scrap of trash from the garbage could be gnawing on a human body part in this hopeless realm. The voiceover provides a haunted internal monologue, a human voice that reacts to the awfulness of his landscape. Frankie is the viewer.

There is an important section of the film when Frankie is accosted by Paco the loan shark and his cronies. We learn that Paco owns everybody. Frankie doesn't own a single thing in the world. He has more outgoings than FedEx. Meanwhile, his wife eats Coco Crispies out of the box as Rikkie screams in a starving mantra. Playing over the tragedy at this point is a conversation between Frankie and his father. He tells his son not to associate with people of colour. Bombs keep crashing. He can't tell where one torture ends and another begins, and neither can we.

This movie is a fucking endurance test and it's amazing.

Everyone is operating with surface desire, one goal—to score, to survive, to escape. Even the rabid but loveable junky Mike has resorted to mugging people so he can pay Paco for a hit. The desolate landscape is interspersed with flashbacks of Frankie in a VC torture cage.

War is the annihilation of everything that is beautiful. Giovinazzo, while presenting an undeniably cynical film, does offer us the hypothesis that war is not natural to man, that it is the antithesis of our need to be free and exult in a sense of community.

Early on, Frankie is stalked by armed natives, one of whom is a beautiful woman. He initially basks in her beauty, even when confronted with a conflict scenario. In the end, his fear is the destroyer and Frankie reverts to fight or flight. He turns around and shoots the beautiful girl. He lowers his gun and watches the slow-motion slump of his target. Frankie is so disgusted by his actions. He drops his gun and runs off through a graveyard of his murdered comrades.

"I'm a hero. God help me!"

BLOOD EAGLE

The world of childhood
was like a drunken dream,
a world without money or friends.
That's when coldblooded dreams of my own death
came in the night,
with heartless regularity.

Dreams always ended the same way,
with me basted in oil,
and my body slung over a gridiron
to be devoured by familiar angels.

But if Thoth hadn't wanted me to dream of my own death,
then why did he give me knives
in the form of words?
And chemical plastic
to play with—
boron, cadmium, and phthalates

to suck on?
And why did he put me in a flat 10-feet-tall from the ground?

Drunken dreams became waking nightmares,
regularly boiled and keelhauled.
He trained elephants to crush my faith,
and I was sentenced to thirty years of white room torture,
and he gave me a paper bag of sorrow in the gut to suppress appetites,
a choke-hold to keep the words in,
an enemy in every mirror.

I knew Nirvana before I ever heard Smells Like Teen Spirit,
music of the Ling Chi.

The only book I had was about Nordic execution.
I remember the Blood Eagle.
The back was slashed to give access to the ribs,
broken and twisted upward to look like jagged exposed wing-bones.
A dash of salt to flavour the blood,
then the lungs were dragged out and draped over the bone-wings,
and I worried about Thoth's ability to read minds,
but I needn't have worried.
Thoth was a card-carrying Scaphist.

But this thing.
Thoth.
What was it?
It had always been there.
My own Chinese execution van.

I didn't realise at the time,
but it was not my enemy.
It was protecting me.
Numbing me to sunsets,
exposing me to the tough love of the Morpheus.
Dragged by horse,
taken to the gallows of brain-buried muscle,
to the bleeding edge of sanity.
So I can bring my dreams of death to life
without dying.

WILL TO POWER

In Rainbow City, madness is freedom and therefore is the most sought-after currency. I watch Freddy Nietzsche, rank with syphilis, dream a new insanity (or more accurately, I watch his self-plastic surgery deconstruct the skin of his old waking life)—a sept wound he has staged, focused with the zoom lens of self-conscious thought. It's no surprise that absurd visions park themselves snugly at the studio of inner-madness. In a textbook of the Right Honorable, five hundred Handsome Men highlanders appear, summoned and swollen with similar syphilitic burden. Freddy mutely thanks them for connecting his collective fantasies, repaying them with nothing more than his eternal devotion of dream-decision.

—Deeper into the mad reverie, we see Weimar.

But can the Handsome Men see a wasteland of kings drowning in creative freedom—from their vantage near the film studio called The Decomposing God? There, execs lie in wait for meaning and prophesy. Chaotic dream investments hang in the balance.

—Duddie, desp'rate beggar, Wi' a knife! Faith, you old wife's tale!

A door opens and we're all invited in. There has been an

abduction. Freddy's dreamscape becomes the crime scene of a thousand kidnapped children. Murderers of all murderers. You and I. The landscape dissolves. Rainbow forests, sun, riverbanks emerge. Freddy composes slow-fictions about Earl Marshal, the serial killer. Because serial killers might bring order to this place. Their insanity in waking life provides logic in our dream life. They can deconstruct this wasteland. This might save us. And Freddy. Our poor Rainbow City. But we soon find out that the Handsome Men have taken on Shakespeare and are less strong for it. Blasted creative dew! What of Buchenwald?

And Her?

And he?

And it?

The Handsome army has failed. Stitching comes loose and we delve to new depths.

***

—At the age of her mouth, I uneasily kiss her body goodbye with my sad brains using EEG. I can never see my wife again.

Rainbow City monitors sleeping people's creativity and measures against recent experiences. Logic adjusts, adapts, and the world makes sense. The packages of prints are prepared for Fred and the Honorable Highland Society—MRI scanners mostly. Scientists who have Unskaith'd by hunger'd Highlan help form new connections between what has been explored in and of the inner surface. It seems Feddy was right above the westbound motorways. Our human capacity to devise photographs of grotesque wounds in a vast desert, where luminous concerts swell and sur la vie death.

A coronation of light assembles around Freddy—as butchers might assemble around the lurid hotel rooms in Erfurt. The instalments of new Rainbow mystics have destroyed this place. We have destroyed this place. The Handsome Men tried to help us find insanity, they really did. And Lord Grant, also known as REM, turns in his multi-coloured grave at what we've done. Now we are happy here. In the Semi-Mad City with mayor Freddy. Not since biblical times, philosophers ans, il faisait des. Des. We try to will our creative chaos into reality. Will it, and today Freddy dies in his last hospital bed.

OIKEIÔSIS, GETTING THE BAND TOGETHER: WITH STEVE FINBOW

You moved away from England when you were quite young, is that right? I'm really curious as to what your upbringing was like. I have such respect for people who can escape the stolid working-class, wage-earning environment, but to this day fear keeps me rooted. Was this what happened when you left for New York, or was it more practical that that—and by that I mean, were you fleeing some kind of oppressive kitchen sink conditioning or did you simply, innocently want to spread your wings? I know discovering Burroughs' *Wild Boys* was an eye-opener for you...

Not really. When I was 21, my girlfriend at the time—who was at art college in Liverpool—gave me an ultimatum, "Leave London and move to Liverpool or end up dead in the gutter." I was drinking too much, taking too many drugs of various kinds; so while drinking a pint of Stella and snorting a few lines of coke, or whatever that shit was we bought from the Hells Angels, I thought about it and decided she was right and so up and left. I then spent the next six years or so at the University of Liverpool. Towards the end of that period, I was teaching critical theory part-time and was offered a full-time position but didn't enjoy academia. A friend of mine was living in New York City and thinking of opening a bookstore there or in Providence and asked if I would like to help him.

How did you eventually come to hang out with Allen Ginsberg and ultimately come to be under his employ? Was he an intimidating presence?

In 1988, I received a research grant from the British Academy to look at Burroughs material in Allen Ginsberg's archives at the Butler Library. I wrote to Allen for permission and he answered and said to call him while I was there. I did, and he said to drop by the apartment on East 12th Street. We chatted and I had a few beers. I returned to Liverpool with a good story. Actually, going through customs at Manchester Airport, I was stopped and searched and the officer found copies of *The Wild Boys* edition with the view of the back of a boy's legs splattered with blood and semen, plus *Dead Fingers Talk* and other WSB books, so I was thoroughly searched and missed my coach. Anyway, a year later, when I moved to NYC, I called Allen just to say hi and he asked me to drop by the new office, which was on East 14th Street, and we talked about what I was doing in NYC. That night, Bob Rosenthal (Allen's manager) called and asked if I would like to research and write the biographies of people who appeared in Allen's photographs that were to be published by Twelvetrees Press. I accepted and then became a full-time researcher, archivist, editor. No, Allen wasn't intimidating at all. His presence was felt when he came to the office, but he was extremely friendly, encouraging and generous.

As an educator in the public system I have to watch what I say here, but I adored *Grave Desire*, your cultural history of necrophilia. People often have a lot of trouble separating the art from the artist: what draws you to transgressive topics and do you ever worry about backlash?

I certainly do not worry about backlash but I don't write books just to provoke people. If people are offended, that's their problem. I usually write books because I am interested in a subject but cannot find books that are related to that subject and so I research and end up with enough material for a book. *Grave Desire* came out of my fascination with taboo subjects and serial killers but also out of my interest in the Marquis de Sade, Comte de Lautréamont, Hans Bellmer, Jean Benoît, JG Ballard and so on. And we have to remember that what is transgressive in some cultures is accepted in others. What is transgressive in one century is conventional in another. What I am drawn to is limit-experience and how humanity blurs, pushes at and breaks through the boundaries of morality, ethics and aesthetics (a sort of anti-aesthetics). So Ted Bundy, Louis-Ferdinand Céline, Otto Muehl, Kathy Acker. When I was young, about the time I first read *The Wild Boys*, I was in a gang that listened to the New York Dolls, David Bowie, Iggy and the Stooges, the Velvet Underground, Jobriath and when we went out we dressed in glam-ish outfits, wore make-up, very transgressive for that era and area. Then I became a punk, so transgression has always been part of my life. Arthur Rimbaud was my earliest punk hero.

William Friedkin's, *Cruising* must have played some part in your research for *The Mindshaft*, but do you have any opinions on Franco's, *Interior: Leather Bar*?

Yes, I re-watched *Cruising* at a glacial speed and think it is a very good film, and there are some great doppelganger moments in it and cinematographic parallels with Jacques Scandelari's 1978 movie *New York City Inferno*, which I am not sure are intentional. I thought Franco's, *Interior. Leather Bar* a good concept but a poor execution. The idea was to make a film of the missing forty minutes of *Cruising*. Franco called Friedkin and said, "I'm trying to make a film about the missing forty minutes of *Cruising*." I (Friedkin) said, "Uh huh." And he said, "By the way, what were the missing forty minutes?" [laughs] I swear to God, he'd been shooting it! I said, "Well, it was just pure pornography that I shot because I could." So it was a pretty pointless exercise and interjected a moral aesthetic which really should be left to the viewer.

I completely agree. I meant to ask: are you musical? Would you ever consider working with other avant-garde artists, like Whitehouse?

I bought a new bass—a beautiful black semi-acoustic Guild—when I moved to France in 2016. I play it irregularly and am about as good now as I was when I was eighteen, which isn't very good. I listen to a lot of music and my tastes have shifted over the past ten years. I've always enjoyed industrial, noise, noise rock and had followed experimental music alongside punk and post-punk—Throbbing Gristle, Cabaret Voltaire, Nurse with Wound. On moving to Liverpool, I got caught up in the Liverpool scene with Echo & the Bunnymen, Teardrop Explodes, the different incarnations of Wah! and also the early days of The Haçienda across in Manchester. In NYC, I went to CBGBs a lot but it was past its best. It's only more recently that I've caught up with the back catalogue of noise, noise rock, industrial bands and now very rarely play punk or post-punk and never listen to the Liverpool bands or Patti Smith, Bowie, Reed, Dylan and such. I like Whitehouse a lot and power electronics in general and I have connections with Philip Best through Amphetamine Sulphate and with Peter Sotos through James Williamson's Creation Books. I find some of Whitehouse's politics a little dodgy, but I think it's a provocation art stance to use fascist iconography and ideas, a shock treatment, similar to those used by bands like Throbbing Gristle, Einstürzende Neubauten, Laibach and also members of the YBAs back in the late eighties. As for working with these bands, yes, I would love to but no-one's asked me. Especially groups and people like Trepaneringsritualen, Merzbow and Puce Mary. And I would have loved to have been the bassist on the nights Les Rallizes Dénudés played the Yaneura club in Shibuya, Tokyo, during 1979, 1980 and '81.

If we weren't in lockdown and living miles apart I'd ask you to be in my band. We could have Zoom jam sessions. What's our band's name? Something high-brow. We could go for *The Wild*

***Boys* and reclaim it from those shameless new wave philistines, Duran Duran?**

Thanks. I'll have to search for my black-sun plectrums, can't remember where I've put them. I'm not very good on Zoom. I dislike video calls. I hated that Duran Duran song and always thought one of the lines was, "Wild boys always shave," but it's shine, apparently. And what's going on with, "Where is all you angels / Now the figureheads have fell?" But our band's name, hmm, yes, something high-brow. Ich/du or Pervitin or Catachresis or Perfidious Geometry or Plane of Profligates or Entr'acte or Zastrozzi; I like Remora Lampreys or Rōdōki (Japanese for 'record of labour' or 'worker's account') or Oresteia but my favourite and close to my philosophy of art is Oikeiôsis. Ladies and gentlemen, I give you Oikeiôsis. Get fucking loud!

CONTIGUITY TO ANNIHILATION

—'This is my El Dorado. Everything I need is in this place, Ivan.'

—'Then fucking go. What do you need my blessing for? What do you need me for?'

—As he stared into her electrically excitable cells, which possessed the power to sooth his tired limbs and elevate his soul, Ivan knew he had lost her.

—'That's not what I meant.'

—She lied.

You can see from this exchange with her boyfriend and bandmate, Ivan, that Marina had left Germany for this place—just off Briarson & Fuller—in the full knowledge of the cosmic threat confined within this innocuous little American town. And she knew deep in that elemental vacuum which sucked at the coil of her soul that these were more than mere rumours designed to unsettle tourists. Scientists and spelunkers alike had returned home as deaf and wounded shadow-people with seemingly evidential reports of malignant entities—photographs and murky infrasound recordings of wandering monsters who lurked in the obscured folds of space and time. Overheard voices that begged for sacrifice in an alien language. So, Marina had to go, didn't she? She was compelled by her art. Her insatiable creative spirit. Ivan may have hated her for leaving, and there was no guarantee Berlin would have her back when this was all said and done, but the promise of a new annihilation sweetened her fear. Her soul was waiting to lose its petals in a wind-blown cascade. Flowers of orange.

***

AMBIENCE MAGAZINE: Marina, Ivan, hi. In the '90s, your music had this kind of dialectical affiliation with rave culture. Do you miss that?

IVAN: Yes and no. It's all merged into this global Internet world and we have to adjust. But I don't miss anything really. Not even Marina.

MARINA: That's just globalization. Everyone knows everything about everything. The holy grail for a music fan, I think, is to hear music from another planet

***

And the little American town seemed relatively normal at first—'normal' being the most suitable adjective since 'normal' usually meant, sub-textually, that there was a concerted desire and effort to conceal malignant truth behind a veneer of flimsy props and stage-furniture. And this little American town—the one just off Briarson & Fuller—stank of artificiality. A complex stage design of charming wooden town houses lined the main street, more Germanic in style than American. The museum and adjoining public library sat like perfect sentinels of upright academic pursuit, not dissimilar to the Kunstbibliothek across from her and Ivan's old apartment in Matthäikirchplatz. She noted this into her recording device and cursed her stupid sentimental longing. She was only two days away from Ivan. Homesickness at this stage was a sign of weakness.

DOUBLE-NEGATIVE MAGAZINE: Do you miss Berlin when you're on tour? Do you get homesick?

IVAN: NO.

MARINA: No.

DOUBLE-NEGATIVE MAGAZINE: I need to be honest; I can't understand a word of dialogue in your latest EP.

MARINA: That's the intention. It's just another way of withholding certain details for yourself. Because you don't know what someone's saying, whereas I do. I know every syllable on that EP. Not that I would expect anyone to care, but it's a way of keeping my privacy.

DOUBLE-NEGATIVE MAGAZINE: I put one phrase into software and reversed it, because I thought that it had been reversed, but that just made it sound... more reversed.

MARINA: Well, I was doing that. We're both German, and it always sounds backwards when we talk. It's probably what attracts me most to working with other Germans. It's one of the few reasons Ivan and I are still together.

***

Quaint family-owned businesses adorned every available corner; the town was unsullied by the empty and aggressive commerce of the neighbouring cities. The townspeople appeared pleasant and quiet, even the young people conducted themselves with admirable reserve. And she noted that the weather was pleasingly warm for spring, and the smell of autumn-blooming native plants filled the senses with freshness and hope for a merciful winter. Marina observed all of this with a keen eye but was not fooled. The town structure was nothing but elaborate cardboard scenery in a complex theatrical ruse. But who was behind it? What was the purpose? She had no answers to these questions but knew that behind every well-behaved mask lay the silent but thickly-present promise of a black hole, albeit masterfully contained. It was here that the music hid dormant but restless, ready to explode in a fit of electromagnetic mellifluence. She and Ivan were performers of some renown in circles where ambient music was held in regard, and it was her search for a field-recording of the unheard pitch, the tunings of evil, that had brought her here. To this town. Forcing herself to face the dead eyes of the townspeople in an effort to extract the sonic source of their ugly spirits. And these raw materials interested her, oh yes. Even if it meant literally *killing* one of them and surgically removing it by hand, she would get her sound. Even without words, the biophony of the town was deafening. What a shame, she thought, that Ivan lacked her commitment. Lacked her courage.

***

SHRIKE MAGAZINE: Your music has always been cutting-edge, courageous, and there's no doubting your commitment to the exploration of new sounds. In most of your newer music, there's a lot of detuned sounds and these very shuddery, in-between sorts of harmonies. Do you remember when you first discovered those sounds?

IVAN: I don't know when I did, but I've always liked and enjoyed weird scales and tunings. I've been using my own scales for quite a long time now.

MARINA: *Your* scales?

An old man who resembled a decaying Brian Eno stood by the roadside observing Marina over the rim of his bifocals as she observed the town. He was wearing an apron and slip-resistant work shoes and leaned against the wall waiting for Marina to look in his direction. Eventually, their eyes met and a cold fear instantly struck her in the pit of her chest. The old man told her to approach without using words. The locked stare brought Marina into involuntary motion. She crossed the road and followed the old man into the alleyway behind the fishmongers named 'Al's Cod.' She assumed this was Al.

' I'm Al,' he said with words. So, she was right.

'Marina,' she replied, still transfixed by the intensity of his gaze. The old man emerged half from the shadow of the alley and Marina could tell that he was not human. Although his skin draped tightly over a human skull and his body was the shape of a standard bipedal mammal, and while he spoke English well and by all accounts resembled an elderly anthropoid...he simply was *not* human. Nor was he necessarily malignant. If it's possible for a being to possess an atonality, then Al would have embodied it fittingly. Al blinked and raised a palm to Marina's cheek. In the spirit of seeking new experiences, she allowed him to do this.

Marina saw in Al's eyes pistils containing nanoscopic glimmers of hope that reflected back to her perfect diffracted holograms of precious nostalgia. In that moment she decided to trust Al implicitly.

'You do not belong here. I can see who you really are. It's dangerous to come here so nakedly.'

'Nakedly?'

'Without camouflage.'

'Well...I'm...here...so...'Marina tried to speak in coherent sentences but her voice was failing her. Her distraction was too extreme. She knew she was talking to something not human and she couldn't stop thinking about it.

'Why are you here,' it asked.

'I'm an artist...'

'Painting?'

'No...'

'No?'

'Music,' she eventually let out. The ringlets around the old man's eyes were like hypnosis wheels and it was clear Al had power beyond cooking fish.

'German?'

Marina nodded.

'You need to pass through to the next town right away. Do you understand?'

'No...I *can't...*'

'You come here looking for a truth beneath the surface. This is not a truth you want to discover. These masks we wear are designed to protect people like you from seeing what really lies beyond.'

'Annihilation...'

'Yes.'

'You are not ready. Your type are proponents of the pastoral psychology and of magical thinking. You seek a proximity to god while indulging death drives and the pleasure principle. We don't have the answers you want or need.'

'Please...do you think...do you think...'

ROLLING STONE MAGAZINE: Do you think technological developments affect the way we create and interact with music and sound art?

MARINA: Oh yes, we can also look at the ways in which alien sounds in ambient music tend to 'conceal' found sounds of far-off spaces. I've heard it compared to bringing a souvenir back from a holiday. Then there's the emergence of ASMR composition, which has begun populating YouTube and creating more accessible ambient therapy. But I'm really concerned with bringing back that souvenir. We need to locate and explore alien worlds first. I think NASA and their space programs should use music as their motivation for terraforming. It doesn't have to be about rebuilding society, it could be about just finding new music instead.

ROLLING STONE MAGAZINE: Who is speaking in your last EP?

MARINA: Just Ivan and I, because we are the only people who exist in our world. We're just back from a tour with House of Rosen, Annalaura Alifuoco and Silvia Battista, but we were always alone. We are all always alone. Ivan and I have tried to focus on the social and political implications of the last EP, why not use it to speculate what an alien world sounds like for the next full-length album? Unfortunately, that is just speculation.

ROLLING STONE MAGAZINE: You are certainly committed.

MARINA: What would be the point in compromising with our music? Even if we are just...speculators.

Sensing Marina would not compromise or reconsider, Al decided to give her what she wanted. Once she saw and heard what lay beneath she would be changed, warped forever into something new and broken. He sighed, lifting both hands to his cheeks, flattening the loose flesh at either side, peeling his fingers around his jowls, prizing away the face like a biscuit tin lid.

It made a *pop* noise.

The first thing that struck Marina was the smell—an ethereal mildew. But the black gaping maw soon stole the edge of her attention. A deep dark hole that extended beyond the dimensions of Al's skull burned in her mind, in her soul, and most interestingly, into her auditory faculties. A drum noise scuttled out of an invisible analogue machine at around 120bpm and joined a tuneless synth in a psychoacoustic ostinato. Marina tried to press the RECORD button on her device but her body would not obey. Children screamed from all corners of her psyche as slime-covered beasts ate her dreams and eventually consumed her dream-parents. In memory, men and women Marina had loved wailed so hopelessly that they vomited-retrograde into their own memory-souls.

'The icy chill of R'lyeh. Can you feel it getting closer? Is this what you want? The truth?'

Marina fell to her knees. The noise ended when Al had reapplied his face lid. Everything was silent. All sound had been sucked into Al's face and she heard the world for what it really was. Silent. And Marina knew her auditory faculties had been stolen, never to return. Was it all for nothing, this loss of hearing? She thought she was ready. Her hand held the recording device limply with her broken thumb stabbing the PAUSE button into the metal frame around the plastic.

So, it was all for nothing.

No evidence.

Only the loss of music and conversation from her life.

She would never hear her mother's voice again.

Never hear David Bowie or Massive Attack.

No more Aphex Twin or KLF.

She would never hear Ivan curse her or say 'I love you' again.

They existed only as vague stereo-spread audio-memory.

Placozoa.

Sickened by this loss, Marina fell silently to all-fours by Al's slip-resistant shoes.

'You are just a young girl. You were not ready.' The voice spoke to Marina from within her own mind. An alien voice, not her own.

'Spermarche, menarche. Ids with swim wings on. And you, Marina, rely on adults with dead children in their eyes to guide you. A parallax. A wreath. Say goodnight into my void, will you?'

Marina felt the organic glue that held her flesh mask in place start to loosen and tear free from the seams. She tried to scream but the voice was lost. She felt her face fall into her palms, landing like a wet glob of gelatine, and looked up with a new voiceless void.

'Goodnight'—she thought.

AMBIENCE MAGAZINE: 'Goodnight' by Soul Tragedy is one of the albums you've independently produced—do you think the band will continue without your partner of 20 years?

IVAN: Without a doubt. Marina's silence has spoken volumes. I know she's out there and as long as she found what she's looking for then I have no ill-will towards her. Well, maybe a little...

DESPERATELY SEEKING ARISTOTLE'S FRIENDSHIP OF VIRTUE

Let's argue that reality is plural: the solipsistic loneliness of individual perception becomes our first hurdle. We try to get over that by sharing some kind of rudimentary interior with others—where common goals and grammars can unite and define us as joint proprietors of a greater cognitive space. So how do you deal with people not liking you? What strategies can you call upon when you reach out for connection only to find an opposing electrical charge exerting its repulsive force against you? It seems strange to imagine that in the age of social-media anyone would reject this idea of a cognitive space of mutual connection, but it's harder to attain than you might think. Well, it's harder for me at least.

It sounds cynical but sometimes, no matter how many ways you attack this complex endeavour with reasoning there is simply no way in. Some people just don't want to share an interior with you. In truth, most people don't. Which means that even if reality is plural, our experience of it is doomed to be paradoxically solitary and singular. Knowing that truth doesn't make the problem any easier to live with. So, is this just the end of friendship for Chris Kelso? The optimist in me says 'no'. The other voices say 'mmm, well…maybe'.

When you write books about critter-states, child murderers and psychosexual trauma, it might seem like other people's opinions aren't all that important to you in the first place. But that's not true. I write to exorcise my sadness and put some distance between my day-to-day self and those grim fascinations. Writing is to be a friend of wisdom. The books are rarely ever an expression of how I feel or what I enjoy. In fact, I have yearned after stable conventions since I was a young boy. Sure (at my lowest ebb, when I felt it had eluded me) I battled against conventional structures, but always in the secret hope that it would eventually come to me of its own accord. Like a jilted lover hell-bent on retribution. An arsenal of mind-games and denial at my disposal. But I want(ed) friendship. I always wanted a good job and the status that brought. I wanted a place in society. Self-fucking-actualisation. And Maslow was right when he outlined his tenets in the hierarchy of needs (although having critical 'needs' will make you inherently 'needy', and this is also unattractive). I want to believe in goodness and an afterlife. I want to believe in romance and meaningful connection. Alas, this is the loneliest I have ever felt. All these conventions continue to allude me and I need to make peace with another harsh truth: my own undesirable status as a fundamentally needy soul navigating the morgue of human indifference. Losing the optimist soul. Accepting the void.

And that's what this is, I suppose—*this*, right here. I'm trying to articulate something so I can connect with someone out there in the great collective abyss. Shine a light on it all. But dark matter only consumes; it neither reflects nor absorbs the light. Only eats it.

Aristotle defined friendship as reciprocated goodwill.

'In poverty as well as in other misfortunes, people suppose that friends are their only refuge.'

Goodwill certainly seems to be in abundance on a superficial level, but does it have genuine truth or is it some kind of trivial social camouflage? If it did then surely connection would be simpler and would occur on a more regular basis. I'm also aware that the materiality of our reality conditions the connection of everything with everything else. I know we are cosmically bound, like the milling atoms of a crystal—interdependent particles oscillating together in the quest for structural integrity. And as I step into a new profession with demanding and stressful challenges, friendships become more important, yet somehow less accidental and more intentional, albeit still fate-pending. Friendship becomes about utility, survival. The kind where there is no real reciprocal affection. Two cold bodies clutching hold of each other in a superficial embrace as they spiral into apathy together. These are usually temporary relationships and these are where I find myself dwelling of late. And usually it's me who needs more. I often try to break this shallow barrier with sincere acts and a giving nature. Because I need the friendship of virtue in my life. Unfortunately, no one has the patience required. My 'needs' appear 'needy'. And my overtures of friendship deflect off chitinous eyes and ears. My gifts of connection pass through transparent hands and crash hopelessly to the floor.

I am lucky to have love in my life. I have a fiancé who connects with me. She represents the world of reciprocity that I craved. But what of fraternity? That's been a different story entirely. But so what? An optimist resides inside my heart, muted but present. I'll just have to wrestle with undesirable status until the black soup of dark matter takes me beneath its well. B.R Yeager once told me that 'humanity sees the void as a vacuum/an absence only because we aren't tuned to perceive what resides there, and as conscious entities we put consciousness on a pedestal.' So, this struggle to elevate consciousness through connection and shared experience is perhaps folly. Dying alone doesn't frighten Yeager because, as he says, 'I imagine my consciousness will just disappear, become other energy, scatter, etc. I won't be aware of it or its ramifications, and that's strangely comforting.'

Maybe there will be something beyond. In the dark matter we can't see. A new world of simple connection and reciprocity. But that's the optimist talking...

VOIDNESS

10 SESSIONS

A PSYCHIC-INTERVENTION WITH COSMIC GUIDES:

EVAN ISOLINE, DOMINIK MILES, JEFF JACKSON, PAUL CURRAN, PAUL KWIATKOWSKI, MATTHEW STOKOE, BEN ROBINSON, DEREK MCCORMACK, AUDREY SZASZ, THOMAS MOORE

A black watery sludge of crippling consciousness sloshes around my head in loose bilge, ebbing and flowing with each panic-surge of electrical energy. The effects soon become psychosomatic: it's an internal sensation that wets my palms, prickles my scalp with fear and fills the already-clogged neural funnels in my brain space with anti-natal thoughts. I wish I could stem the torrent of noxious bilge water, even for a moment. My head feels constipated.

Session One: Evan Isoline

Drugs can help. But I don't like drugs. And I know what most people's fantasy image of escape is: all wired up to some virtual-reality headset, interacting with an augmented reality through motion controllers and sensors while a chemical compound of essential nutrients filters through your veins from an IV drip off-shot. But I'm looking for natural relief, and if terror management theory is to be believed then mortality salience is achieved through high levels of confidence and self-esteem. Alas, I have very low levels of self-worth, and therefore am highly motivated by my fear of death. My cultural anxiety buffer is down, my immune system depleted and open to the viral horrors of the world that shake my cells to their very proteins. My only freedom is in distraction, in forgetting. Self-deception, if you will. I wander into the local greengrocer in a psychogenic fugue state and I see a man I recognise. A man who can distract me.

Evan Isoline runs SELFFUCK, an intriguing online journal that promises 'masturbation, ontological violence, ambiguity and transmutation,' and it's easily the most consistently interesting and confrontational magazine I've come across in years. You can't find his zines at my local corner shop. You need to plug into the Matrix to access it. Evan also works tirelessly making immaculate boutique zines that re-ignite interest in the flickering wick of human experience. These aren't available at my local corner shop either. I was interested to hear about Evan's first experience with the call of the abyss and if the 'voidness,' as he calls it, ever threatened to engulf him. I walk up to him as he's placing a bag of heavy hass avocados on a groaning scale. My mouth starts motoring as if possessed by an excited demon.

Evan? How are you? You're well?

(Evan can tell I want to talk about self-fucking from the desperate look in my eye)

I...

If I seem a bit wired it's because I wasn't expecting to see you and I'm doing this book about the abyss.

Ok—

Evan doesn't make eye-contact but I have him in my emotional vampire-tractor beam.

Now, to 'fuck', I tell him not with words but with extrasensory waves, ***is to seek sexual gratification from the fissures of another person/ or object. For men 'self-fucking' is probably simple onanism, intellectual or corporeal—pulling at the buffing machine until it manufactures a bleeding jewel of your essence. Self-pollution to some. It is the ultimate distraction process. Until it's over. Now, self-fuck could also mean to 'love oneself'. I mean, what other act of appreciation is there than masturbation? In the book of the Iliad, Homer declares, "Give me masturbation or give me death!" But if I were more cynical then I would probably believe the metaphor means to self-indulge. Marx condemned the entire field of philosophical study to masturbation. And if that's the case then I am a master self-fucker. It is a process all creative people are in union with, I suppose.***

You know, I first felt the call of the void when I was 6 years old.

Oh yeah?

My parents and I were on our way to the Island of Arran. My dad took me to the stern of the ship so we could see the contours of

the oncoming island as we approached. It was this vague misty image in the distance and I wasn't that interested in it.

No?

No, I was too busy glaring into the toothed V's of the Atlantic water beneath me, the great propellor lapping and churning in mesmeric hymn against the metal shin of the vessel. I gazed into the grey water. Looked at the thruster. All I could think about was clambering over the stern and throwing myself into the blades below. Cut up and spread apart in a watery grave only to be dragged mainland by fisherman and port police. It scared me. It felt unnatural. I didn't jump. I am a predictable person who respects the life bestowed upon me. But what was that urge? A Freudian death drive. Maybe. I've had several experiences like that since and it gets harder not to jump every time.

Well, did you have a conventional upbringing? Does Arran have some kind of weird Scottish 'Wicker Man' thing going on? Maybe you were pushing against something? Here, wait till I put these avocados back in my trolley.

Not really. There is a holy island though, but the monks are benign and I never visited. I mean, was *your* upbringing conventional?

My upbringing was quite fantastic in terms of family. I was however extremely shy and sensitive as a child, not really knowing why, which caused inevitable anxiety and depression. Getting older I've found much value in solitude, silence and observation. I relate spending time alone to the experience of voidness. I relate the empty page, stage or canvas to voidness.

I recall that Dutch movie, *The Vanishing*. The serial killer, Raymond Lemorne, jumped from the balcony of his home when he was 16. The fall broke his arm and fingers, but he felt he had succeeded at 'pushing against' what he felt was preordained—that he *wouldn't* jump. It could be that same push, the need to defy the preordained and the familiar. The safe. Do you ever think about it in these terms?

I'm not so sure, but it's important for things and people to become intermittently empty I think, or to empty out and encounter states of emptiness. To me, voidness is a vacancy that gives way to fullness, voluptuousness and dimension. It is something beyond the temporary and permanent, beyond good and bad. Voidness is something omnipresent, indivisible, and endlessly generative. Because being alone is not typically perceived as a discipline or a virtue, however, it comes as no surprise that people are taught to be afraid of it.

Do you find comfort in this 'voidness'?

I find comfort in that getting to know myself has been more of an active process of deconstruction and unknowing. These ideas extend to what I'm interested in doing in my own writing and publishing projects as well. I admire art that is multidimensional, mysterious, and attempts to utilize or understand chance. I think there's great joy in artists sharing space in a way that utilizes darkness as substrate or a stage where new things can be discovered based on the idea that new chances can be taken and unforeseen performances made. You should speak to Dominik...

Thanks, man.

Dominik. Dominik...I scroll through my phone for 'Dominik.' Then I remember my Dominik. I type with all the ferocity of juiced existential anxiety. I was following some kind of celestial breadcrumb trail set up by cosmic guides. First Evan, then Dominik Miles. I need to try and talk less.

Session Two: Dominik Miles

(Picking away the protective layer of a scab on my elbow. Nervous displacement? The phone rings. One ring. Two rings. Pick up.)

Dominik Miles, hey. It's Chris...

Chris...?

Kelso...

Oh...sure, Chris. How are you, man?

I was sent to you.

By?

Forces beyond our control or comprehension.

Ah...

You started SCAB magazine recently and it deals with homosexuality and art in a very nihilistic way. You seem like someone who isn't afraid of nothingness...

As far as I can remember, I've been terrified of nothingness! As a child, I didn't have to face death too often, but I still had seemingly bottomless anxiety about suddenly being forced to leave the only state I know and enter something that might be—nothing. Growing up, my fear has gradually shifted into other dimensions, and now, it mainly manifests itself in the terror of the possibility of carrying death around in one's body, unknowingly.

Are you an optimist then?

Are paranoia and optimism mutually exclusive?

I suppose both are healthy in moderation. What brings you comfort in the terror of silence?

Anything that breaks the general silence or seemingly breaches the fine walls of this very specific silence tends to give me comfort. I'm deeply drawn to everything damaged enough to be half here, half somewhere else. I'm fascinated with people reaching their extremes—physically, mentally, etc.—and art born from these experiences. I like going as close as possible—but only as a spectator. I forever want to remain a voyeur.

Is nothingness just an unconceptualized space in our subjective reality?

Session Three: Jeff Jackson

Narcolepsy is another burden of mine. I'm standing on the platform of an eerie train station. I can't remember how I got here, but I am mid-speech. Sleep drunk. I think I am alone. Silent Hill-esque fog surrounds me, and I feel the weight of on-the-nose dream symbolism. Jeff Jackson, a remarkably well-established—though affable—Californian who has struggled intermittently with the voids' bleak absorbing gaze, overhears me speaking out loud. He's sitting on a bench waiting for his own Amtrack to enlightenment. There is a moment of pause between us. I shake off narcoleptic fuzziness. I don't recognize him at first; that's the way with narcolepsy—amnesia before clarity. The first lucid thought that comes into my mind when I eventually register his face is, 'Jeff Jackson deserves better than this...'

Which void are you babbling about exactly? *he asks, folding up his paper into a neat quarter-pamphlet.*

I, uh...was I talking about the void again?

There seem to be so many—the abysses that originate from the outside and the ones you discover within yourself, the abstract philosophical concept of oblivion and that incredibly personal sense of crushing emptiness. So many relationships, so many different maneuvers required to keep from being swallowed by a sense of utter hopelessness.

Can I sit here?

Sure.

Are you an optimist?

While I tend to be pessimistic about people and the state of society, I think optimism is embedded in the act of making art. Without some deep innate sense of optimism, I know that I wouldn't bother to write, spending countless hours trying to get the sentences and structures just right, convinced this matters on some level beyond ego and commerce.

So, what else is there?

Extremely pessimistic writers like Samuel Beckett and Thomas Bernhard created some of the most well-wrought prose of all time. Their negative vision is paradoxically built on a foundation of belief that the project itself is worth significant care and effort. For me, their work offers a more profound optimism than authors whose books may be sunny on the surface but whose shoddy quality reveals their ultimate cynicism.

I hear a train coming and so I stand up but suffer sudden cataplexy. My body flops from the platform and I fall in deluge onto the sleepers of the train line below. Jeff is nowhere. Sleep envelopes me. Hello Abyss. Again.

Session Four: Paul Curran

Some of us have the abyss thrust upon us. Take Paul Curran, author of Left Hand, for example. In narcoleptic dreams I recall details of our last conversation. He was wearing a gaberdine overcoat over a tactile turtleneck. He had oversized shades and a fake nose. Paul was on another mission.

Paul, you're leaving?

Not exactly...

So you ran away from the UK?

As a juvenile, I was sent from England to Australia for crimes I didn't commit. The ship took six months and was infested with rats. Sometime later, I killed my girlfriend in a car crash. After spending six years in an institution, I was deported back to Britain and advised by a discredited Harley Street psychiatrist to relocate to Japan.

And your mission?

My mission was to bring back the penis of Kichizō Ishida, which Sada Abe famously severed after the autoerotic-asphyxiation murder of her lover and carried around in her purse, as depicted in Nagisa Oshima's (1976) film *In the Realm of the Senses*. According to Schreiber (2001), the organ was preserved and kept in the specimen room at Tokyo University Hospital but went missing after WW2 when it was put on display at the Tobu Department Store in Ikebukuro, where I'm currently employed at Rikkyo University. So far, I've exhausted fictitious leads pointing to the Steely Dan III from Yokohama in *Naked Lunch* (Burroughs, 1959) and fabricated spurious connections between the Setagaya Murders and the Rainbow of Light, an Aum Shinrikyo splinter group. But my relationship with the void remains convivial. As Roland Barthes (1970) said in *Empire of Signs*, which was referenced in the original French title of the Sada Abe film (*L'Empire des sens*), Tokyo has an empty centre. This is also what Gaspar Noé (2009) was referring to in *Enter the Void*. The imposing architecture of Tokyo most associated with images of Shinjuku that influenced *Blade Runner* (1982) makes me forget about my own mortality. My wife grew up in Shinjuku and used to mess about jumping between buildings while I was walking around somewhere on a beach.

I feel the sleepers cold and hard against the back of my skull. More questions than answers really but I wonder if he ever completed his Kichizō Ishida mission...

Session Five: Paul Kwiatkowski

I wake up in my bed. I have a headset on and the heavy bouillabaisse of self-awareness leaks into sharp focus. I have a feeling akin to some wicked mouth abscess. Receptors are ringing. Inflamed pulp. Fear of oncoming night terrors. Dry sockets. Awareness of the wisdom tooth. Jig-saw pieces of memory fall into place post-cataplexy. Voices are reverberating in my ears. Two men in somniloquy. A podcast. Another sign?

Paul Kwiatkowski wrote a lovely coffee table book called 'And Every Day Was Overcast' and he doesn't get enough credit for it. He now holds reign over my favourite podcast, Wake Island—a venture which he finally does get sufficient credit for. This podcast is like real company, the kind I dreamed about when I was a lonely teenager. I get the kind of fraternity from Paul and his Wake Island guests that I couldn't achieve through face-to-face communication. I struggle with direct interfacing, so I've always enjoyed vicarious community access. Paul offers me verisimilitude, a waking dream with writers I admire. Here I can be a passive, guilt-free observer. He is the enabler I prayed for. We merge in the collective conscious to chat.

I grew up in Loxahatchee, a rural and secluded part of South Florida. The isolation had a sense of violence to it. There was no culture or reprieve from ignorance. I never met my neighbours. South Florida was the end of the line. It was where people came to die, evade the law or get away with something. I grew up around people who had a lot to hide. I think about the movies I watched in high school: *Fight Club, The Matrix, Wild at Heart, True Romance, Badlands,* and *Natural Born Killers*. Looking back, walking away was my favourite trope. Throughout my adolescence, I was obsessed with escape.

I can't say why, but you seem like a man who likes to plunge himself into the vast existential ravine. When was your first existential panic?

My first existential panic was having a family member die of AIDs. I remember the secrecy, shame and lingering sadness that hovered over my family. I remember conflating love and sex with death at an early age. Watching HIV play out in pop culture started to create this rift between myself and reality. I couldn't comprehend it. Within the isolation, I spiralled out into depression. It took me a long time to process all that and reorient myself.

We are all equals in thinking about death, and we all begin and end thinking about it from a position of ignorance, but what brings you comfort in the terror of silence?

Life is a state of free fall. We can fall together or we can fall apart. Either way, we're heading for impact. One day, our thoughts and bodies will become an abstraction, we'll exist only as ideas and as the trail of media we leave behind. To avoid despair, I think it's important to find experiences that take us outside of ourselves. There's great comfort in articulating ideas that feel ineffable. It's the only way for us to make sense of the abyss.

Do you think podcasting that deals with darkness directly can have therapeutic advantages for the creative soul? It helps me tremendously. It keeps me anchored to the world, imbues me with some sense of social-purpose.

Before I started *Wake Island*, I wanted to slow down time. I desperately wanted to crack open the monotony accumulated over hours and days spent scrolling through timelines. I started to notice how quickly time passes when we're pacified by technology, rarely alone with our thoughts. I also felt that those memories didn't count as experiences or interactions. That sense of desperation has been compounded by the pandemic.

You're also a nice guy who is probably sensitive to changes in environment—do you wrestle with that odd and intrinsic urge to pursue transgressive conversation/art? Which writers give you the most relief?

I wanted to engage writers I admire about tone, atmosphere and aesthetics. I believe that the intensity generated by transgression has momentum that lives on and expands over time. I love it when a writer has gone someplace they can't come back from. The writers that give me the most relief are the ones that create books that have an immersive atmosphere, a headspace that isn't totally bound by convention and codified messages that you can enter into and leave transformed. The ones who write books that haunt us long after we've confronted them like *Cows* by Matthew Stokoe, the George Miles Cycle by Dennis Cooper, *Eden Eden Eden* by Pierre Guyotat, *The Consumer* by Micheal Gira, and JG Ballard's *Crash*. Right now, so many of us are feeling the disconnection brought upon by quarantine and COVID. We need transgressive art to jolt us out of our stupor by pushing us beyond the parameters of everyday life. We need art that reminds us that we're alive.

I think I might be tired of the constant reminders.

Hey, man. Since you're here, would you mind looking over something for me? It's kind of a multi-layered surprise.

Intrigued, I agree and Paul offers to show me a short film he directed called Dog in a private occipital theatre of my own creation. The screenplay for the scenario was written by Matthew

Stokoe. A projector flickers into life and Stokoe appears fully-formed as camera obscura right in front of me. He looks at us from behind a pair of aviator sunglasses. Silver hair slicked back over an undercut. Stokoe is a private man but he reluctantly agrees to meet me in dream-manifest thanks to Paul. Our silhouettes engage in a shadow play against the anterior wall.

Session Six: Matthew Stokoe

Stokoe starts talking without being prompted. He is an oracle. A telepath. The perfect dream-guide.

If by "the void" you mean that construct which we use to discuss questions about the nature and meaning of existence, then my upbringing left me sitting firmly on the edge, dangling my feet, peering down.... I'm not sure how much room we have to "manoeuvre" here. Wondering about why we are here, what happens to us after the death of the physical body etc. are questions that are pretty fundamental to every self-aware being on the planet. Once you've identified yourself as a distinct entity, separate from everything else around you, then you kind of have to ask what your role is. If you accept that, then each and every one of us is engulfed by the void as a condition of (self-aware) existence.

Are you an optimist? Do you still experience existential panic in spite of your pragmatism?

I'm optimistic in some things and at certain levels, and not in others. I will admit, though, that I find musing about existence an experience often tinged with the bitter fizz of anxiety.

Do you think you get closer to any kind of closure as you approach the final days?

I'm not sure that we all, always, end our days as completely ignorant of the meaning of death as when we started. In some sense, surely, life is about trying to figure out why we stop living. Currently, what gives me comfort is the hope that some part of us exists elsewhere and that death is not a turning-off but a shifting of awareness, from one vantage point to another.

What motivates you to create? Are you working on anything at the moment?

Money, the garbage other writers churn out, a love of euphony in language, the satisfaction of achieving a complex and elegant structure, the need to think about and examine certain bits of life and the world, the need to fill time, a desire to dodge the guilt of having wasted it.... And, no.

Stokoe pushes me out of my own mind...

Session Seven: Ben Robinson

I watch god interpenetrate every aspect of being, abstract and physical, in one motion. Ben Robinson is telling me that his own upbringing was happy and safely unremarkable suburban normality all the way, raised by cool left-wing parents, an art teacher mother and an electrician father, who were into cooking and free jazz. I relate to everything except having parents with taste. I hear another Scottish accent...

Since adolescence I have aimed to somehow rebel against this way of life by turning myself into a cliché via courting oblivion. This would be done through the usual Rimbaudian systematic derangement of the senses, and later via art and culture which might bring about this perfect high in its own unique way.

And after art school?

After the art school life I began working full time in a call centre, its own kind of cliché in turn. I have also worked as part of a group producing an art zine, later making my own art, films and texts. I was diagnosed with MS back in 2002 and have been discovering new landscapes within myself each day ever since. Thankfully, the constraints the disease has put upon my body have not affected my capacity for independent thought. For this I am grateful.

It must have been challenging—has your diagnosis altered your relationship with the abyss, beyond a more acute awareness of your own mortality?

The void has made itself apparent to me at several points in my life, but I have found that the most effective way of warding off this malevolence is simply by doing things. Even my answering these questions negates death. I define myself as being broadly optimistic.

Session Eight: Derek McCormack

In the fall of 2011, I nearly lost one of favourite prose-stylists. Derek McCormack was diagnosed with a cancer in his digestive system, for which he underwent extensive surgery. He came out the other end a well-dressed wound, and he's brought some souvenirs of wisdom from the ether.

We meet in an abandoned fairground called 'Joyland'. I've never been here before but I know things about this place, intrinsically. Every busted ride tells a story. I realise the reason I know is because I'm sharing cognitive space with Derek McCormack. He shows me the rusted tilt-a-whirl that detached and cut two little boys from Connecticut clean in half. A Flying Bob that flew straight into a tree, impaling the poor Miller family within. A Spinning Teacup and a Scrambler that spun and scrambled many neighbourhood children into pink smoothie.

What was your upbringing like? As a cancer survivor, what is your relationship like with the void and has it ever threatened to engulf you or can you manoeuvre around its dreaded omnipresence? Can fashion save us?

I want to thank you for asking me about death—death's something I'm really good at! I'm never not thinking about it. A few things comfort me: junk jewellery—rhinestones, gold-plating, silver-finish, fake nacre, pinchbeck garbage. And I also like prescription drugs.

Are pills a type of jewellery?

Yes, of course—everything's a sort of jewellery. My cancer's an accessory—it's very rare and very desirable. No, that last part's not true. The truth is that I'm cancer's accessory: it wears me. I had cancer scares when I was a kid—I have memories of multiple cystoscopies. I'd get strapped to a gurney with my feet in stirrups and then I'd get gassed asleep—when I awoke, I'd piss blood. I spent decades preparing myself for a catastrophic illness—and then, when it came, a couple of friends said that it was the big break I'd been waiting for, as if I were Lana Turner and cancer were the casting director! Which means the world is Schwab's Pharmacy! I loved that. I'm a hypochondriac. I was raised to be a hypochondriac. My maternal grandmother taught it to me: she kept a Merck Manual beside her bed and regularly diagnosed herself with dreadful diseases. She taught me something else too: fashion.

As an introvert who thinks silk-screened novelty t-shirts and bargain bin corduroy is acceptable attire—I need to know: am I beyond saving (even in a fashion sense - in that I have no sense or comprehension of fashion)?

Well, my grandmother wore Eva Gabor wigs and Day-Glo polyester pantsuits and the gaudiest goddamned costume jewellery. The trinkets drug stores sold. It occurs to me today that her hypochondria was a prayer for health and her fashion sense was a sickness. In any case, it was sickly. Sickening. What if the jewellery she wore—the paste pendants, the plastic pears—was really a way to draw death to her, to turn it on? What if the fashion she wore—the fake furs, the tawdry wigs—was a sort of death that immolated her and made her into Eva Gabor, or Eva Gabor's ghost, or her dead twin—a Gabortion? There's no way it's that simple, though: I don't think fashion is a type of death; rather, death is a type of fashion. So her fashion was death that dressed up as death. Who wouldn't love that?

Session Nine: Audrey Szasz

Sometimes I think being an only child connects you more with the abyss. You grow up more selfish and aware of yourself. You get to reflect and dedicate that time to focusing on your own neurosis. What do you think?

Well, I was born in Vienna to expat parents, and I'm an only child. My parents were from quite different backgrounds, and they moved me around a lot while I was growing up so unfortunately I attended a few different schools and lived in a succession of very boring places.

Sounds very similar to mine. Once my mum got a job as a doctor we moved out of the slums and enjoyed a very sheltered and comfortable lifestyle.

I was subjected to a mentality that was basically very middle-class, conservative, or petit bourgeois. So in some respects my upbringing was unusual, but on the other hand, it was probably not that remarkable in the sense that my parents were white-collar workers who watched the television every evening and read the newspapers. They listened to the radio. Their general views and outlook upon life reflected the conformist mainstream media they habitually consumed. My mother bought my clothes for me, fed me, and made me do my homework. She made sure that I could speak English (the world's lingua franca) and gave me plenty of books to read.

Were you creative as a child?

I always had a sketchbook to draw in and a set of colouring pencils, etc. No matter where I happened to be living, my home was situated in a clean, orderly environment. I was even provided with an Xbox at one point. So I can't really complain to be honest.

And your relationship to the void?

In terms of the void—well, it all depends on an individual's outlook I guess. Without wanting to state the obvious, I'd have to conceptualise the void in purely metaphysical or metaphorical terms. And in some ways it's like a Rorschach or a word association test in that whatever I answer will doubtless reveal much more about my mode of thinking or my character than this so-called 'void' which I personally consider to be an absence, or an emptiness, or a meaninglessness.... It's therefore paradoxical that I'm being asked to conjure this 'void' into existence by engaging with it as an abstract, theoretical concept which in practice plays no genuine role in my day to day life, because no matter how much I daydream or ruminate, I am grounded in my physical needs and sensations. And then there's my brain chemistry, neurology, the question of consciousness, etc.... But these are philosophical issues as far as I'm concerned.... People such as Jean-Paul Sartre, or Albert Camus, or even Viktor Frankl (just for example) have pondered at length over such topics.

But you...?

But as far as I'm concerned, I appear to be alive, I appear to be conscious and I appear to possess a degree of free will and the ability to operate within certain parameters (i.e. within the observable laws of physics, etc). I know by now what I like and don't like and I apparently gravitate towards various sensations which for one reason or another I find pleasurable.

Are you conscious of the limitations of the reality in which your consciousness interacts?

I'm obviously limited in the sense that I'm a human being and my species has apparently evolved on this particular planet in this particular galaxy, etc. In a way it's very easy to survey the universe (or in my case read a textbook or watch a TV show presented by a scientist who's decided to helpfully explain everything 'we' currently know, etc.) and regard humanity as totally insignificant. Is that the all-encompassing void? Or is the emptiness within? Ultimately, everything anyone ever does is basically pointless. Or is it? Does it even matter? I feel as though this void, or rather, the conceptualisation and analysis of the void, is inherently ambivalent.... But it's my personal analysis right, and that's what counts?

Subjectivity....

Yes, and in any case, I can't help seeing everything through the anthropocentric lens.... My conception of time and space is seemingly regulated by the fact that I'm living in the northern hemisphere of a planet that rotates every 24 hours and takes 365 days to orbit around a star, etc....

What about the limitations of language, are you consciously aware of it when you're trying to articulate your subjectivity?

When I write, I'm writing in a human language and I'm limited by it. Or perhaps a better word would be *contained*.... So we live within the confines of our bodies and senses, and our environment, etc.... I really feel contained by the apparent materiality of my body and the objects that surround me, and by my perceptions, my thoughts and feelings or the images in my mind's eye or the languages I might use to communicate.... And all of that adds up to quite a lot in terms of counteracting the void.... If I exist right now, that's enough, I don't need anything more. I don't wish for immortality because I think it's worthless. I don't know any better and it's probably impossible to know any different. To me, this entire question is simply an intellectual exercise....

No dread?

I don't feel any sense of dread. Maybe I'm just dead inside, an emotionless husk? Haha. But seriously, I can accept that there is an inherent absurdity to human existence and it doesn't really bother me anymore. And you know, I could have answered this in many different ways.... I could have taken a completely different stance.... But I've basically just written whatever unfiltered thoughts came to mind....

Are you an optimist?

Sometimes. But my attitude towards life is often quite fatalistic.

How so?

I'm aware of the limitations of various belief systems so I can weigh up my options and cherry-pick in terms of what attitude I'm going to take regarding a given situation, although ultimately I probably just do what is expedient, which is arguably quite cynical, or I default to self-pity. Having said that, I really dislike hypocrisy for some reason so if I do cheat a little bit every now and then I won't do it behind everyone's back, it'll all be out in the open. I'm basically on a life-long quest to surround myself with enablers. Just kidding! Sometimes you have to cut a few corners.... Sometimes you have to burn the candle at both ends.... One thing that I do really like (apart from idiomatic phrases) are deadlines. That's very important in my line of work.... I push everything back until the very last moment and I enjoy the pressure. I feel optimistic enough to know that I'll always pull something out of the bag. I am lucky enough to know what I'm good at, what I enjoy, and what sort of things I'm genuinely suited to, and as for the rest, I avoid it as much as possible....

What about when we're done here? Does anything await?

Well, if I assume there's no life after death, no reincarnation, no continuity, no human soul, etc., then I guess I won't be conscious so.... I won't be aware of it anyway. I can't remember anything from before I was born so I figure death might be something like that.... I don't really want to die at this point in time. If I do happen to die in the next five or ten years, then it'll probably be caused by something unavoidable, something I can't control.... I don't think I can find any solace.... Just denial or cognitive dissonance. If I was about to be executed, I would start off by trying to be cool about it and act all casual, but in the end I'm worried that I'd probably just panic and start crying like a baby. It's hard to say really. Facing one's own mortality really does put things into perspective. So much of life is trivial and meaningless. It's easy to get wrapped up or carried away.... But when you're facing death you realise that very few things are actually that important. Life is too short, but it's also the longest thing you get to experience.... Dying seems so easy but also very difficult at the same time.... So I guess this means that, if anything, I personally find comfort in clichés and truisms? I can live with that....

Session Ten: Thomas Moore

And now I am in such a deep state that I know I am inches from death. I know this place as the Great Abiding Lonely. Ben Lazare Mijuskovic said loneliness is not primarily about an inability to relate to others, rather, a by-product of self-awareness, independent of intersubjective development—but to be aware and isolated even in death? It's like being buried alive. Does that mean there must be something fundamentally wrong with me? My efforts to quantify the hearts agony never abates. And I wonder what state Thomas Moore was in emotionally when he wrote Alone—in my opinion, the great 21st century novel about the spiritual phenomenon that plagues us all in our private moments. It seems like such a raw nerve of a book. Thomas had one of the toughest upbringings imaginable and while his art is bleak, his outlook isn't. I ask his living reflection if he thinks negative experience is important when attempting to create worthwhile art.

It was a couple of years from when I started it to when I finished it—which probably seems crazy considering how short the book ended up—so I suppose my state changed a lot over that time.

And when you're writing?

When I'm actually writing, I'm pretty much in a meditative state—I kind of imagine that's what it's like for most writers. There's an inner silence and a neutral feeling in a way—everything stops. It's hard to fully sum up, but there's no other state like it. I don't have to be in a negative space to write. I don't have to be in a negative space to write darker stuff or a happier space to write happier stuff. I do think that pain plays into stuff but it doesn't always correspond time wise if that makes sense.

I've always felt somewhat estranged from the domain of the soul, but never went through the kind of turmoil you were subjected to. What was your upbringing like?

The sections in Alone about the narrator's childhood were borrowing certain facts from my own. I was physically abused and severely neglected as a baby and taken into care by Children's Services, and then luckily adopted and moved away from all of that. I was raised in the suburbs.

Would you change it if you could? Did it have any bearing on the artist you became?

My family didn't really know how to communicate that well with each other, but I was forever grateful that they rescued me from what my life could have been, so despite anything, I know that I am lucky. I definitely had what would now be recognised as some kind of attachment disorder as I grew up. That stuff will definitely have played into my work in a lot of ways, I'm sure. I don't know what I'd change ... I find it healthier not to think in those kind of ways—the fact is I can't change it so why waste that energy? In terms of life getting to an engulfing stage—I've certainly had bouts of depression and all of that but it's all relative. I feel lucky to have writing. I don't know how people who don't have art can cope.

And who inspires you?

I tend to get inspiration from visual art, music, film, just as much as I do from writing. I could probably make a list of visual artists and records that have influenced and inspired me just as much as books have. But thinking just in terms of writers.... and I need to preface this by saying that it would probably be different on any given day, so this is not definitive and also as soon as I read this back I'll realise that I've forgotten some favourites and get mad with myself. But for today, off the top of my head: Marguerite Duras, Joan Didion, Lawrence Ytzhak Braithwaite, Tim Dlugos, Eileen Myles, Dennis Cooper, Maurice Blanchot, Georges Bataille, David Wojnarowicz, Alain Robbe-Grillet, Peter Sotos, Mark Gluth,

Derek McCormack, Bret Easton Ellis, Jelinek Elfriede, Philip Best, Ariana Reines, Travis Jeppesen, Dodie Bellamy, Kevin Killian, Lynne Tillman, Elaine Equi, Edouard Leve, Alistair McCartney, Pierre Guyotat, Blair Mastbaum, Robert Pinget, Robert Siek, Scott Heim, Elle Nash, Christopher Zeishchegg, Lindsay Lerman, Chelsea Hodson, Anthony Dragonetti, Josh Peterson, New Juche, James Nulick, Dale Brett, Martin Bladh, Audrey Szasz, Elaine Kahn, Shane Jesse Christmas, Chris Kelso, Golnoosh Nour, Jeff Jackson, James Baldwin, Paul Curran, Grant Maierhofer, Brontez Purnell, Gary Indiana, Bo Huston, Colin Herd, M Kitchell, Kathy Acker, Douglas A Martin. I've missed off loads I can tell and I already hate myself for it. I'm sorry to all the genius writers that I've forgotten to list!

That's a good list. We are all equals in thinking about death, and we all begin and end thinking about it from a position of ignorance, but what brings you comfort in the terror of silence?

Art. Friends.

And with that, I sleep. A dark, soundless sleep.

VISITING HOURS

*

The world opens its eyes,
breathes in acrid chemical.
Light enters in a burning slingshot of negative mass and energy.

**

Quantum slipstream subsides.
Sight adjusts.
The world looks around, absorbs the sterile room.
Sees IV tubing connecting the world to apparatus.
A heart monitor connecting it to machine.
The pumping hydraulics of an oxygen tank in its left ear
connecting the world to the industrial soundscape of a futile rebuilding process.

***

The world remembers how it got here.
And with that memory comes a sharp pain
in the left temple of the world.
Instinct compels it to raise a hand to the skull to nurse the wound,
But neurons fire to dead limbs.
The world cannot move.
A lumpen, lead heap of trans-planetary matter.

****

So, the world buries its fears in a deep silent place
where decades of pain rests obese and dormant.
A mother's shame, a plugged duct,
A wasted nipple.

*****

The world drags its gaze to the ceiling and tries to communicate to its enucleated children.
It burns the stare into something telekinetic.
A concentrated refrain travels through the air and to the collective conscious.
A mercy plead from victim to perpetrator,
mother to typhlotic son.

******

The world asks, 'When are visiting hours anyway?'
No one replies.
Visiting hours are over.
No children bothered to come by.

POINTLESSLY DEVOTED

I've known Jordan Rothacker for almost a year now. He was brought to my attention after reading a fascinating article of his in Entropy magazine. It focused on his best friend who died of a heroin overdose in 2016. Three years later, Rothacker would embark on a pilgrimage of sorts, to St Louis where he would transport his friend's ashes to the gravesite of William S. Burroughs. It was a powerful piece. Powerful enough to make me seek out Rothacker on social media. We haven't looked back.

His novel, *My Shadow Book* is an example of a 'nested novel' that (stylistically) meets somewhere between Burroughs' early SF-infused fragmentations and the wisened meta-charms of Alan Moore or Iain Sinclair. The premise may seem somewhat prosaic, but the cumulative patchwork is both complex and enlightening. Jordan A. Rothacker places himself at the center as facilitator—a 'double agent' who stumbles across a box containing the journals of a mythmaking being known as 'Maawaam.' Rothacker succeeds in making a poignant and resonant statement about the nature of art, the prison of art, and the plight of the hostage artist. Maawaam is driven, yet dour and directionless. The fact the book feels cohesive is a testament to the writer. It's fantastic, really. Rothacker's new book, Death of the Cyborg Oracle, is a heart-aching death note to our philosophical and spiritual future.

Rothacker currently lives in Athens, Georgia where he received a MA in Religion and a PhD in Comparative Literature from the University of Georgia. He also received a BA in Philosophy from Manhattanville College in Purchase, New York, the state in which he was born. His essays, reviews, interviews, poetry, and fiction have been featured in such publications as *The Exquisite Corpse, Guernica, Bomb Magazine, Entropy, Vol. 1 Brooklyn, Brooklyn Rail, Rain Taxi, Dead Flowers, Literary Hub,* and *The Believer*. Rothacker is the author of the novels: *The Pit, and No Other Stories* (Black Hill Press, 2015); *And Wind Will Wash Away* (Deeds, 2016); *My Shadow Book by Maawaam* (Spaceboy Books, 2017); and *The Death of the Cyborg Oracle* (Spaceboy Books, 2020); and the short story collection, *Gristle: Weird Tales* (Stalking Horse Press, 2019). 2021 will see Rothacker's first non-fiction collection, *Dead Letters: Epitaphs, Encomia, and Influence* (Reprobate Books).

Your novel, *My Shadow Book,* occupies a strange artistic space. You place yourself as facilitator or archivist rather than 'writer'—for a work so beautifully-written, was it difficult losing the 'writer' credit and assuming one of 'editor?' For most writers, it's unthinkable to remove the ego. It seems like a brave creative sacrifice. Are you someone truly devoted to Trocchi's commitment of exile? Art above all else at any cost?

Well, certainly not above all else. I don't have that deep selfishness that I've often worried is required to be a great artist. Or maybe it is discipline instead of selfishness I lack? This of course ties in with the construction of *My Shadow Book*. Through method acting, it became almost a passive writing experience. And that is also why such a short book took me years to write.

And the ego?

And as for ego, it's still my book, so if anything, that separation of myself from the work is a failed conceit. But a fun one. But it also ties in with some of the disillusionment in the book, and which ultimately led to the creation of the book. That struggle with the emptiness or pointlessness of art. Art is a thing that is so special to me, that makes me feel so excited about life and the potential of humanity, and quite often it falls on deaf ears, and artists feel like we are creating in a vacuum. I know I'm not alone in this. So, the book is to speak to that, and to reassure others who feel that way. It is the closest I'll ever write to a self-help book, but that is what it kind of is, like a pep talk for artists and activists.

So, if we could stay on *My Shadow Book* for a moment: Maawaam, while driven mad by the process, is an entity who really revels in the fantastic possibilities of achieving authentic art. I think about Michel Houellebecq saying, 'We need a supreme antidote against all forms of realism.' Do you agree with this? Does art still have that power in a world of over-saturation and a society's complete immersion into the *jouissance*?

Haha, like old Uncle Bill, "Storm the reality studios!" I might share Houellebecq's sentiment, but with an inverse of semantics. Recently, I have been picking at a manifesto of art (not that *My Shadow Book* isn't its own sort of manifesto) and it's all about extreme realism and anti-genre. There are lines like, "Everything is real. Everything matters. The role of art is to convince everyone of this," and "Extreme naturalism includes unicorns, aliens, and gods," and "If a book jibes with your feelings of mystery in the world, how is that not realistic?" As we in this woke 21st century global society seek to expose and lessen binary thinking, genre in the arts needs to find a way to the chopping block. Particularly, in the Anglo-American literary world, the obsession with keeping fiction and non-fiction clearly defined and separate needs to be cured. But I do worry of art's power.

With the oversaturation?

Well, yes, we are oversaturated. There is just so much. So much shit, sure. But there is also so much great stuff. What worries me most is a generation raised on the internet that has access to all of this information and actually accesses it, but has no education, and by that I mean understanding of context. It is information that never becomes knowledge and is then doomed to never contribute to wisdom. It might be the dumbest post-modern actualization of Hassan I Sabbah's, "If nothing is true, everything is permitted."

Could the truth be that realism is adulthood, the loss of child-like ignorance and bliss? Therefore, adulthood must be hell, or some equivalent? My younger friends love to

debate the mechanistic materialism of H.P.Lovecraft. His work is accessible and appeals to their youthful fascination with the macabre. And Lovecraft was, somewhat notoriously, a man unable to transition into full godless adulthood, much like myself; a state of being congealed by a series of private inadequacies. As such, his characters tremble with the same inadequacies. But, of course, Lovecraft was a pretender, a false heir to the throne of nihilism and chaos. His theories are thoroughly inconsistent.

Doesn't Ducasse joke about that in a letter, when he is ready to let go of the Comte personae and publish his *Poesies* under his own name?

You know, I'm not sure...

His second—and final—work is his mature, reverent one. Of course, he subverts all of that through detournement. I think that you, especially in your recent work, show a sense of maturity and certainly an open-mindedness and wisdom that has surpassed Lovecraft. He was a bit of a one trick pony and maybe crippled by his own narrow worldview. I think the most original thing in his work—and I might be wrong, and someone else did this first—is the idea that human beliefs, myths, and fears all go back to an Ur-myth that came from outer space.

How much is Rothacker and how much is Maawaam?

The writerly answer would be that it is a totally fictional creation, but all me, as all the characters I create come from me, out of me, and are me. But this writing process was one of method acting. I developed this character out of my own pain and frustrations and then gave him life in his own journals. When I thought thoughts that fit him, I wrote them in there. That journal—which became several journals—was always in my pocket and I wrote in it out in the world. The text itself bleeds in and back out of reality and life and the clues within it support this idea and crazy experience. References to Anna Kavan and Rimbaud's "Je est un autre" tease out the lie that Maawaam is me and that he isn't. Also, for the narrator of the text, becoming Maawaam within the book is just as much a twisted process.

I have a deep love of Jean Genet. Notice I didn't say "Genet's work," or "Genet's work and life," because he is one of the greatest examples of an artist whose life and work is almost impossible to untwine. A journalist at *The Guardian*, Tim Keane, who reviewed a collection of Jean Genet's art writing described it perfectly, so I'll quote him entirely: "Genet's moral universe interprets reality and human actions as inherently, if subconsciously, *purely performances*. To him, the failure to understand the preordained aesthetic motivation within every act is the basic source of our misunderstandings about how the world works. And it is our moral failure. Art may not be redemptive, he suggests, but its primacy should be our main priority. He interpreted his whole life, even the most mundane or vile experiences, as high art."

You know, if we think about Lautréamont's work, could Maldoror be described as a protagonist of Lovecraftian

motivation? It is not so strange to say it—after all, Lovecraft and Lautréamont share a theodicy, a kind of inbuilt cosmicism that permeates their work.

I definitely feel connections in their work. And it is more of a feeling of something shared, and you might be right about a cosmicism. However, there is a bravado and swagger to Maldoror—maybe it's his Frenchness—that seems unthinkable for a Lovecraft character. I can't imagine any character in Lovecraft's oeuvre having sex with a shark. It's such an amazing scene. Also, the confidence behind Maldoror's utterance, "Si j'existe, Je ne suis pas un autre." It's a coincidental reversal of Rimbaud, but such a strong assertion of selfhood and sovereignty.

TIDAL RIVER

WRITTEN WITH GIO CLAIRVAL

Tidal bores occur when a wide, flat estuary surges upstream against the natural flow of the river's current, causing the incoming tide to form a breaking or undulating wave. There are only around sixty of these phenomena in the world, eleven of which occur in Great Britain.

Glencaple, Dumfries and Galloway County, Scotland

A cold month of September. Late afternoon and darkness was already descending outside the church. Like strobe lights, dust swirled before the sconces on the walls as I stared glassy-eyed at the casket.

Reverend Kilgore, pale skin, lined and dry like parchment, cleared his throat. Thick, black-framed glasses perched on the bridge of a large hooked nose. The minister shuffled papers on the lectern and several strands of greying hair fell forward across his forehead, betraying the extent of his comb-over.

Please, let's just get this over with, I thought.

My mother, dead. She had been acting out of sorts long before she killed herself. Growing up, I remembered her as a completely different person from the emaciated creature who wasted away toward the end of her life. Mum had started having monstrous nightmares but when she tried explaining them to anyone we thought she'd gone insane—*and you could hardly blame us.*

"Finn," she would say, "have you ever felt fish scales moving under your skin?"

I would say, no, Mum, fish scales can't get *under* your skin.

"You're wrong, love. Every woman can feel them. Sometimes they sooth you, sometimes they prickle you so hard you want to scratch yourself until you bleed."

In the church, the reverend paused. The silence brought in the noise from the outside. My little town was in deluge, gobbing out giant reversed teardrops with the size and resistance of Kalamata olive pits. Through the rose window, I could see steam rise from the river below, around the gloaming streetlamps. Something about the weather made everything unreal.

I sat in the front row between my father and Daniele, my little sister. My father's grief showed with the downturned corners of his mouth. So embarrassing. Old people shouldn't display their feelings like that. Weakness didn't match his hatched-carved face. Despite the abyss of time his features were weirdly similar to mine; but Dad was a sketch of existential helplessness. So unlike me. Certainly, my gothic appearance was out-dated and some found my cool disaffection tedious, but at least I had the resilience of character to keep my emotions in check for the sake of family.

Dad brushed forefinger and medium against my elbow. The rough texture of his fingertips made me shiver. I wished I hadn't picked this three-quarter-sleeved black dress. I wished

I were already wearing my thick coat. The air smelled of moisture and damp mushrooms even indoors. Walking into the church I'd had the impression of wading in the river.

I pictured myself surrounded by tossed water. Maybe, if you opened your mouth and swallowed the Nith River's salty water, scales could crawl inside you. After a minute things like tickling feathers would come to the surface, just under the deeper layer of derma, and move toward your heart. Because the heart pumps your blood like the moon pulls water, and tidal rivers are strong, conflicted and secretly violent.

Mum lashed out when no one would listen to her rambling. At some point she began to paint wiggly tattoos all over her body—strange, complex symbols and cyphers. We asked her to explain what these drawings were, but she simply couldn't answer.

"It's a feeling, it's just a feeling, in here...in HERE..." she'd repeat again and again. By this stage Mum had completely retreated from our affection. It wasn't long before she was dead.

Mum said they'd come for me next...

The minister was reading from his notes, passages from scripture that failed to penetrate my inner world.

If my mother's death still seemed unreal, the cause was perhaps even more so—suicide. Mum had gone from being the bedrock of my life to a black hole that could never be filled. But the dreams were the worst.

Reverend Kilgore droned on, his words a series of formless intonations. To me it seemed I was removed from the scene, as if an invisible divide separated the man in the pulpit and me. I started, afraid I'd been sliding off to sleep, but it made no difference. The minister's words continued to melt the moment they left his mouth, decaying further in transit until they reached me as formless blobs of sound. I glanced at my sister's wide, teary eyes and then Dad's sad grey face.

I felt removed from them too, the only one who couldn't hear the words. And I didn't care. The reverend reminded me a little of the voices from my dreams who talked about cosmic beings, both celestial and abysmal, until I sensed the creatures peering out at me from between the creases of a watery dimension. The incense smelled sour.

***

After the confined atmosphere in the church, the raw wind engulfed me like a cape woven of icicles. Billy was waiting but I wasn't in the mood to deal with him or his shifting habits—one minute he loved me, the next he didn't want to commit.

Fuck that shit.

Billy reached in to hug me, introducing the lingering smell of rain onto my black frock, something that only succeeded in irritating me further. My tongue lapped at an imprint of carcinogenic toothpaste he'd left behind.

Judging by his dishevelled appearance, he'd been drinking. Again. I only wanted to swallow icy water.

Billy, dragging his flaccid fringe back into the mound of dark shag, adjusted his tie (but only made the knot looser, messier), and tried to get all the words out of his mouth before I could walk away from him.

"I'm sorry," he stammered.

I glared, waited a moment, and then collapsed into his arms

like a boneless corpse. Ten steps away, the river was preparing to kiss the sea. Billy held me close repeating that he was sorry, over and over.

Dad came out of the church with Daniele. Mr. McNail was a great heap of a man, eyes scored through with memories of the clandestine military operations he'd been constituent to. He didn't approach me, for which I was grateful. Dad didn't like to see me around Billy, despised the boy; a stranger would think this thoughtful father allowed me to have my private moment grieving with my boyfriend. As if I'd confide in that unstable young wreck. Truth is my father only wanted to keep his little girls away from other men.

Safe.

The sky had gone from grey to a hot silver; quarks of daylight broke through. Once the rain had ceased, the road that ran parallel to the Nith River was left like a shallow torrent, like a sickly younger brother to the greater river. The surface of the Nith trembled, announcing the surge from the sea.

Dad glanced upward. "We're having a new moon tonight." He scrutinized the surface of the water, which quivered with wavelets, silver triangles on pitch black.

Since we moved from Glasgow to Dumfries and Galloway ten years ago, my father had been fascinated by the tidal bores. The highest tides occur during the phases of a full moon or new moon, when the gravitational force of both the sun and moon reinforce one another. I'd learned that the largest annual tides happen around the Spring Equinox in the month of March, and the Autumn Equinox, this very month of September. *Right now.* My skin itched.

Dad's eyes shone with expectation. In his pupils I glimpsed the reflection of two sickles, the moon's crescent.

As a child, I admired my father, but growing up I'd caught a strange expression on my mother's face when she listened to his endless rants and explanations. Professor McNail, she would call him. I didn't understand her animosity at first, until I met Billy and learned how, in so many ways, a man could disappoint a woman. But Billy at least was young, inexperienced. I was his first girlfriend, and I had to tell him what to do and how to do it, instructions which he followed by the numbers. Dad, though, had several lovers before meeting Mum, and—I'd grasped from veiled allusions—after their wedding, too. It was either egotism or a simple lack of empathy. Maybe these two go hand in hand. The McNail women were unlucky, is all.

I thought about Mum, what she was like *before* the transformation; remembered her shock of black hair. A vague portrait of her soft, warm features. What had broken her exactly, I did not know, but if I could have foreseen what would happen to her she would've savoured her smile even more before it disappeared completely from her face. What if those slimy creatures really were out there weaving through the folds and creases of the water? What if everything Mum had said turned out to be true? *Scales like feathers.* Would she have still died for nothing?

Maybe this 'sickness of the soul' was an inherited characteristic that just needed time to gestate.

You're daddy's little girl, no one else's. No one else's...

I pulled my woollen coat tight around me.

"It's here," my father's ecstatic voice whispered.

I stumbled down the short slope onto the riverbank. Small

waves mussed up the water. The surge came rolling in, a meter high. I let myself slump down, my back against pebbles and stones. Somewhere behind me, Billy cried, "Gosh, it's getting huge!"

The advancing bore front rose to double its usual height, but instead of carrying the murky colour of slime the water shimmered as if covered with a film of kerosene. The undulating ripples hurled forward at great speed and left the bed of the river to veer toward the bank.

"Finn, come away, come away!" Billy, again, his voice fading in the distance. Daniele's muffled scream.

Closing my eyes, I waited.

***

The breaker knocked me out for what must've been a good few seconds. My mind retreated to a familiar place, back in my room. In my sanctuary. Safe. But it didn't last. It couldn't. I'm a McNail woman. We're all destined for a tortured fucking existence.

The shadows came, dark, twisted bulges streaking my bedroom walls, bloating, growing limbs and retracting into hollows until the silhouettes coalesced into one single physical form. Now I was being cradled in the arms of some slimy sonofabitch. I knew then that there was no way it was Billy who'd come to my rescue. Arms roped into clusters of bunched muscle, pectorals tensely twitching with each step he took, he carried me with ease.

I knew his smell. Citrus and sweat. I'd known this scent since I was little. The big man had carried me that way all my life.

Before I knew what was happening, the stabbing muscle of a tongue penetrated my mouth and filled it with a saltwater tang.

Heavy breathing through gill-slits. Fluid fingers worked my breasts, penetrated my cunt. The sheen of slime lubricated me, easing the entry.

The estuary opened around us. Webbed feet wadded through the curtain of sea, down the narrow, steeply sided gorge. I was meat being delivered to starving monsters, the same starving monsters that captured my mother and raped her mind. A seagull cried out to the empty dome of sky, an unnatural and confused plead for something, probably the first time its endless hunger had been forgotten. Grey-backed salmon gasped for air on the shoal.

The stink of ammonia tattooed itself on my senses. A rotten womb of sky and sound. The man dropped me into the water like a trawler returning a net full of lost boots to the sea.

***

Flotsam. I swirled with the flood.

I sensed them before I could make out the silvery shapes. Eel-like creatures coiled around my legs. Smooth tentacles stroked me. Questing cilia probed my flesh. Silky flakes. Scales like feathers.

White sparks exploded behind my eyelids. The ocean roared in my ears and sang a cleansing tempest. My mind was left full of light.

The fish-god skin, which I accepted (and my mother refused), enveloped me—a steel-strong armour.

I leaned through the waves like the figurehead of a ship.

The tide hurled me upstream. I raised my arms and led the surge.

THE ANTI-PORNOGRAPHER: FROM DANNY WYLDE TO CHRIS ZEISCHEGG

It's no secret you left behind a dazzling career in the adult industry. How have you found shaking off any stigma in your writerly pursuits? Have there been any hostile responses or sniffy detractors? It must be tough shaking loose the image of Danny Wylde.

Yes, once upon a time, I was that porn guy, Danny Wylde. My first real books (let's not mention the first)—*The Wolves That Live in Skin and Space* and *Body to Job*—were so much about the porn industry. I was only able to write them because of my experience as a performer. Both books were put out by Rare Bird, which had an imprint that dealt exclusively with sex writing. Oriana Small's *Girlvert*, probably the best porn memoir ever written, came out through Rare Bird.

So, the audience for that kind of book was not going to give me shit for having done porn. It was like, "Here's a book about sex, published by a press that puts out books about sex." There was no stigma attached.

But I felt that I wasn't operating in the right sphere, if that makes sense. Of course, writing is mostly a solitary thing. But once the work is out there, it's nice to find your peers, see what other people are doing, understand your work in a broader context, etc...

When I was writing books about porn, I kept getting introduced to other sex writers, or people who had done sex work and happened to write as well. I remember sitting on a panel at some queer lit event. It was like being grouped together with people who went to the same high school but who had nothing else in common. It just didn't make sense. With *The Magician*, it's been a little bit different. I'm incredibly thankful to my publishers, Philip and Sarah at Amphetamine Sulphate, for having allowed me to cross a bridge into this relatively new and exciting small press scene. I assume your book exists in this space too, though I'm not as familiar with your publisher.

Yeah, Black Shuck put out The Dregs Trilogy and they're primarily a horror imprint.

But I think you know what I'm talking about: Inside the Castle, 11:11, Expat, Nine Banded, Apocalypse Party, Infinity Land, etc... There seems to be a devoted literary community that revolves around these presses and the authors they publish. There's a certain shared sensibility. It feels a lot, to me, like the music scenes I grew up with. And no one, that I'm aware of, has bashed me for my porn past.

Like most quintessential rubes, I often conflate sex or public displays of nudity with shame and an excruciating self-consciousness, even though rationally I understand and accept these things as a perfectly natural part of the human experience. How did you silence that voice in your head when you first got into the industry—as a thoughtful and self-aware artist, I assume you have/had similar neuroses (but maybe not)?

I was nineteen years old, and the perfect combination of rash and in-need-of-money. I'd eased myself into the idea by 'modeling' for gay art photographers, most of whom asked me to get naked. A minority offered me extra money to suck my cock. I mean, I applied for regular jobs. But the managers at bookstores and coffee shops weren't getting back to me. I was in school. I needed to pay rent. Plus, at that age, it felt good to be paid for sex. I grew up relatively shy, pseudo-depressed. All that typical teenage shit. It was an ego boost to be told that I had a nice ass, or cock, or whatever. When the opportunity came to fuck girls for a living, it seemed like a good deal. In hindsight, it's all quite embarrassing. I don't think anyone should be made to watch themselves have sex. To see yourself mid-orgasm is a horrifying thing. And I lack all manner of body positivity. I'm no longer young enough, or in good enough shape, to strip down like that.

What is your relationship like with the industry now that you have some distance from it and your reputation as a transgressive writer has been somewhat established? Is pornography something you could see yourself returning to?

My retirement from porn—from performing, anyway—was abrupt. I've written enough about it and don't feel like repeating myself. A quick Google search should suffice for anyone interested. But it was very much a 'my-life-is-falling-apart' kind of thing. In short, I quit performing overnight. But I still had to make money. I'd been in the adult industry for eight years. Porn people were the only professionals I knew. So, of course, I went to my friends and colleagues to ask for work. I was offered gigs as a production assistant, video editor, etc... I worked for several years as a content manager for James Deen.

It wasn't all terrible. But behind the scenes, porn was often grinding, monotonous work. Production hours were long. There weren't any unions, so you could end up on set for 16 to 18 hours without being paid overtime. Editing was mostly a race to get as much done for as cheap as possible. So, I'd scrub hours of hardcore footage on a daily basis. When you're not aroused, sex is just repetitive motion. It's boring as fuck. Editing made me hate porn. Maybe hate's too strong a word, because I think there are some lovely people, friends of mine, who work in the industry and who are proud of what they do. I respect that. But casually, I'll say that I hate porn. I might take an editing gig if I need the money. I won't ever go back to performing.

Can you tell me about the work you're most proud of?

At the present time, I'll go with *The Magician*. I feel like it's the culmination of this horror/auto-fiction style I've been trying to pull off for the past ten years. It's also the documentation of a very personal process. I took all these identities, like porn star and other things that were important to me in my twenties, and killed them off. Maybe the more documented parts of me still exist for the rest of the world. Like, I assume I'm still on PornHub. But to me, this feels irrelevant. Danny Wylde is another person. I don't relate to him anymore.

There's also a lesser-known visual aspect to *The Magician*. I worked with director, Matthew Kaundart, photographer, Gina Canavan, and producer, Luka Fisher, to create a photo series and short film based around the novel; around creating the novel, too. Due to the COVID lockdowns, we've had limited ability to screen this work, but the film has played at some online film festivals and such. There's a photo book available on my personal website.

The visual material was very important to me in the beginning. I may have failed in terms of the scope I'd first imagined. It ended up being financially impossible. That said, I'm proud of the little film we ended up with.

Which artists inspired you growing up? Have you always been a transgressive kid?

As a teenager, I was very into underground metal. My aesthetic is probably most informed by that world, music and artwork from bands like Converge, Neurosis, Wolves in the Throne Room, etc. In terms of literary work: I remember discovering Bret Easton Ellis and Ryu Murakami in high school, and being excited by those books. In my early twenties, a friend recommended that I read

Frisk by Dennis Cooper. That book blew my mind. It was full of all this scary sex and violence, but mixed with teenage longing, and attempts to express the inability to articulate extreme emotions. I'd never been exposed to anything quite like it. I devoured all of Cooper's novels shortly thereafter.

My book, *The Wolves That Live in Skin and Space*, is probably my clunky attempt at ripping off Dennis Cooper. As far as being a 'transgressive' kid, I feel like that word kind of changes with the seasons. In a broad sense, yes, I was attracted to books and film and such that dealt with extreme sex and violence, which is what's typically labeled as transgressive, as far as I can tell.

What are your goals as a writer? The Magician is gathering some incredible reviews and momentum, but would you like to elevate your status to a wider audience, or are you happy with your clique of devoted partisan?

Regardless of what happens, I plan on writing novels for as long as possible, at whatever pace I'm able. Right now, I'm interested in abandoning auto-fiction and working loosely in the horror genre. I've been thrilled with the feedback to *The Magician*. Again, I'm grateful to Philip and Sarah at Amphetamine Sulphate for being this catalyst, in a way. For me, I think they offered a legitimacy to what I was doing. Even though they operate a very small press, there's a consistent quality to the work they put out. The audience trusts them. And I'm a part of that audience now. It feels good to be with a publisher that puts out work I want to read.

Do I want to elevate my status? I've given up any pretense of wanting a career as a writer. From my vantage point, it seems impossible if you want to live outside of poverty. Of course, there are ways to subsidize this—teaching and so on. But my career is in video production and post-production, something I actually enjoy (for the most part) when it's not porn. My desire to reach a wider audience has mostly to do with my interest in the visual possibilities of my work. I went to film school. I wanted to make movies. I'd be lying if I said I didn't have hopes for film/video adaptations in the future. I don't think it would make sense for the books I've put out thus far. We'll see what happens.

CRIMES OF INDIFFERENCE & THE BARBARISM OF LOVE

"One does not become enlightened by imagining figures of light, but by making the darkness conscious. The latter procedure, however, is disagreeable and therefore not popular."

— C.G. Jung

This is my first journal entry, my first contribution to the great airborne anthology of names and stories hovering over the city.

Being a shadow is a funny thing. You flit between the interstices of light all day long and try to project yourself as far as you can, like a shrill squillo over a loud orchestra. It's a lonely life—I don't think people appreciate that. I am merely a tracing on the wall, camera obscura.

Every day, for as long as I can remember, I have watched my light-brother, my sunny overhang, try his damnedest to outrun me. Whenever I turn a corner, half expecting to come face to face with the man himself, he shifts into the nearest sunlit street.

He does this because he knows I can't get him there. I'm like a time delay, always three seconds behind actual events. The lobotomised Jonathon, who basks in the golden dawn, serene as an eagle, thinks me a coward. We can never be friends, he and I.

Now, his rejection hurts a lot, it does, but I think I understand it. He sees me and thinks *Christ, that's a lonely, pathetic existence, eh? Loitering in alleyways, running scared all the time...lonely, unloved...no identity to speak of,* and he'd be right. The bliss found in ignorance, in belonging, is so seductive a prospect that to continually deny it becomes a maddening form of torture. My architect made me this way, made me resolute, made misery a part of who I am. Indifference seems to be a crime, which is a shame because I am forced to feel.

My light-brother, who has a full set of fingers on each hand and a happier frame of mind than most, knows if I get half a chance I'll consume him, *assume* him. I'll fill his heart with darkness and doubt; I'll kill the glimmer in his eye once and for all. I'll do it proudly, efficiently and with a broad smile on my face because the truth is I'm stronger than he is, even though he treads on me daily, hourly. *He's* the one who is always running.

Dazzling flames throw intensely dark shadows.

I'll make my light-brother remember every shitty thing that's ever happened to him since we both came stumbling into existence. Tattoo it on his soul so every time he looks in the mirror he'll be reminded of our story. Because I think he forgets.

But I know that no matter how much he seems to fight my presence, deny it, he *knows* we are intimately linked by a shatterproof bond, because—wherever there is light, there is darkness. He lusts for my darkness as much as I covet his inner glow.

I'm not special, shadows never are. *Everything* casts a shadow. The presence of a shadow does not always indicate the echo of something alive. After all, a fucking toaster casts a shadow. A corpse casts a shadow.

I'll keep dwelling in the night, when everyone else is asleep. I'll hang out in places most people are too terrified to venture. My girl and I can survive if we bring our darknesses together.

I feel that, somehow, my life alludes to all these fairy tales that are embedded in the collective conscious; specifically deriving from a genre you'd call 'science fiction.' There are all these names of writers looming over me, Philip. K Dick, Samuel Delaney, Isaac Asimov, and Octavia Butler...all recorded in the filing cabinets of memory storage. The agglomerations hover spectrally in the atmosphere, floating in a shared pool of configurable computing resources.

I was born with these stories already in my head. I remember more from them than I do events in my own life. I am a prisoner of fiction. I use it to shape me.

I see names drift by, buried deep in the filaments of the cloud—Rick Deckard, The Shrike, Offred, Hari Seldon—all men who have seen their own gods and were able to live a real life because of it. They are fictional characters, shadows, but are as real as their creators.

The great science fiction artwork of David Meltzer, Ganesan, and Hannes Bok float by in composed ice crystals...

But these stories, they're significant somehow. As if these are the writers of *my* story, of every story ever told or worth telling. Christ, it seems as if my life has been steeped in falsehood, boiled down to a series of tropes and clichés that I've been inextricably bound to in the process. Every day I meet a Dick Turpin or a Dr. Benway—whoever *those* people are! The part of me that feeds on this sadness will always be more concerned with Scottish football.

Well, whoever they are, I feel like they are important to the canon of literature inscribed on my limbic system.

A sheet of cirrostratus covers the sky. The names disappear and my head empties of all its retained contents. I imagine Burroughs patrolling in the sewers of the mind, fuelling the virus of language.

I remember something of the old world, before the city. Before there was such awful love.

UMBRELLA MAN

I show up on sunny days
Remote-controlled umbrella man
Slink into focus with umbrella shield
To keep the burning eye away

The marksman and the slave

I'm not from here, you see
Photosensitive, alienated umbrella boy

'They' send me down to take care of things
Take aim
An assassin slave and the motorcade
Locked in an embrace until the sun goes down
Born in subterraneous night
Alienated from nature.
Alienated from my work.
Alienated from you.
Alienated from myself.

The grassy knoll is a mute testimony
To an intelligence far greater than your own
Sensitive, servile umbrella people

MATTHEW STOKOE: ADVICE

As a burgeoning writer, it's important to know the landscape and to conduct yourself professionally. Like any industry, publishing is a big ugly money-starving motherfucker, and you need to know how to survive out there. Be 'brave' and 'insane;' be mindful of frauds, hacks and swindlers, of course—but make sure you never settle for anything less than you deserve (if you're serious about being a full-time writer that is). Getting 'in' though, well, it's all about who you know...

I've called up Matthew Stokoe to ask for advice on how to find and promote my niche. Careful, my insecurity is all over this chat.

In *Words from the Wise*, the question posed to each author is: "A young author comes to you seeking advice. They're riddled with insecurities and completely overwhelmed by the publishing industry. What are your Words from the Wise?"

Novice writers all think they're going to be picked up immediately by a major, by Harper Collins or Random House etc., and that they're going to get a half-million-dollar advance and start doing TV interviews, maybe sell the film rights to Hollywood. It's natural. Writing a novel is such a monumental achievement, the writing of it should be enough. Trouble is, it isn't. This thing you've created, this stack of pages, this collection of your own blood and pain and fear and hope, this thing that is so REAL to you, doesn't really exist until it's out in the world. Until it's in the form of a book that others can read.

So what are the options once you have this stack of paper? Would you recommend the emotionally-turbulent process of submitting to publishers, or is the self-publishing route safer for the ego? Do you think self-publishing still has that stigma attached to it? Does any of this even matter?

You can do this yourself, of course, in paper format through companies like Lulu, or in ebook through Amazon/KDP and multiple others. But you don't want that. Not when you've just finished your first novel. You want the legitimacy, the kudos, the bragging rights, the vindication of having someone else, someone in the publishing industry, an expert in the field no less, deem your book to have met the secret, subjective and ever-changing criteria that separate the amateur from the professional. You want someone other than yourself, your partner and your granny to shout to the world YOU ARE A WRITER! THIS IS A REAL BOOK!

What about agents? I don't have an agent. No one will return my emails. I can't tell if it's held me back or given me independent momentum.

So, until you're forced to rethink this paradigm, you're left with no choice but to find a publisher. And to do this, unfortunately, you're almost certainly going to have to get an agent—a process that, in the majority of cases, will provoke suicidal ideation on more than one 3am awakening. I'm not going to tell you how to find one, because I don't know. Though I have had agents in the past, I don't know . One thing that I do know, though, is that you will be a million miles ahead of the game if you get yourself an "in." What's an in? An in is something that everyone else doesn't have.

So schmooze, basically?

It might be something as banal as having Facebook friended the wife of a literary agent a couple of years back because you liked the pics she posted of the organic wool sweaters she knits. By the time you've finished your novel, you alone, then, of all the hundreds (I'm not exaggerating) of writers querying that agent that month will be able to start your email with: "As a friend of your wife and a fellow admirer of handmade woolen outerwear, I wonder if I might take a few minutes of your time...."

Ok, not the best example, but you get the point. Any connection you can make in the world of writing and publishing may, one day, be something you can use to make an agent pay that life-transforming little extra attention and respond to your query with those glorious words: "Please provide three sample chapters (double spaced, Times New Roman, no attachments) at your earliest convenience..."

Two points here. One, it's actually my personal opinion that social media is next to useless as a marketing tool for an unknown writer or for forming connections with people deep enough for them to bother helping you. You need to do more than just friend people. Two, and pay attention, all agents are not equal. Some are good, honorable, talented, hardworking people. And some... well, they're just fucking criminally useless. So research them. This is your life we are talking about here. Literally. If you want to be able to support yourself financially, and if you want your books to reach the number of readers they deserve to reach—if you just want to get published, for Christsake—then choosing an agent who is too lazy, uncommitted or inept to sell a book that could otherwise have found a buyer may mean you end up pumping gas for forty years instead of having sexy book-nerds queue up to ask for your phone number at readings.

***

On to publishers. My warning above applies here too. Many, many times more so. Agents don't generally sign you to long-term exclusive contracts. Publishers do. The starting point for the life of a publishing contract is usually the length of copyright. I say the starting point, because contracts should be open to a certain amount of negotiation and even a novice writer (via his/her agent, of course) should attempt to limit the period during which the publisher has rights to his work. I've generally not had too much trouble whittling things down to around seven to ten years. If things go well with the publisher, you can always extend your agreement. But if it should happen that the publisher is no longer promoting or effectively selling your book, you'll at least have the opportunity to take your work back and start selling it yourself.

But even seven to ten years is a long time to have to suffer a publisher who does not perform as you would have them perform. So it behooves the novice writer to choose wisely. I opened this piece mentioning Harper Collins, Random House etc. And this is where, in your imagination, as you slog your way through your tenth rewrite, you'll no doubt see yourself starting your publisher quest. But this may not be the best thing for you or your book. There is no point submitting your work to a publisher who simply does not publish the kind of book you've written. All that's going to happen is you're going to get a gut-freezingly demotivating rejection letter. And you're going to get plenty of those anyhow from publishers who do publish your type of book. Finding the right publisher is your agent's job. His knowledge of what all the various publishers are looking for is why he charges his 15%, and this knowledge is one of the things you should look for when choosing him or her.

By the way, the other two important things to consider about an agent are the number and strength of his personal connections to key players in the publishing industry; and his knowledge of contracts. Unless you're a contract lawyer yourself, you'll rely on this knowledge to protect you from unfair or disadvantageous clauses in your publishing contract (it's not unheard of, though, for an agent to hand this off to an attorney).

Now, it may be that the major publisher you daydreamed about as you wrote your book, after being approached by your agent, actually does accept your book. Great! Congratulations. But what if that doesn't happen? Because, you know, there's a really, really, really good chance it won't. Well, this is when you start working your way through all the other publishers out there. But don't despair. It could be a good thing to be published by a smaller publisher—you may get more attention from them and, if you don't write mainstream literature, they may be able to better target a niche audience for you.

A few paragraphs back I suggested the new writer to choose their publisher wisely. This is sound, obvious, common-sense advice. The only problem is, that for a lot of writers, even writers who have published a book before, it can turn out to be meaningless. Because, after having spent two years, three years, five years writing your novel, and then another year finding an agent and then maybe another two years looking unsuccessfully for a publisher (and this timeline is by no means unrealistic), when someone does finally say 'yes,' it will seem, and understandably so, that you and your agent have succeeded in locating the only company on the planet who is willing to take a punt on your book.

When this happens, no matter how good or bad the publisher, it'll feel like you have very little choice indeed—either to go with them, or to spend another unknown number of years checking your inbox twenty times a day for emails from your agent.

I suspect the majority of writers will grasp at the immediately available straw. And who knows, it may turn out okay. You get your book into print. You can start legitimately telling people you're an author. And maybe the book will take off and the publisher will actually be good enough to pay you your royalties. But if things don't turn out okay, you're a long time stuck with someone else controlling this beautiful thing that you poured so much of yourself into. To see what you've created, what you know is a good book, what you know should have made you successful, being mismanaged to the point where you get nothing back from it beyond a few copies to show your friends... Well, that's the kind of thing that can end up destroying a writer.

***

So how do you make the decision? How do you decide whether to go with what appears at the time to be your only option, or to hang tight until some point in the future when a more enlightened publisher—maybe—enters the market? Well, that's something you'll have to figure out on your own—there are just too many variables and it's too personal a choice. But here's something to think about...

Publishing is about money. Editors and publishers love to crap on about art and culture and giving society a voice, reflecting the zeitgeist, etc., etc. But underneath everything, publishing (and agenting, too, in fact) is a business, and businesses exist for one reason and one reason only—to make money. Don't get me wrong, I'm not suggesting at all that you force your writing to conform to this dollar-driven ethos. But when you understand that the publishing business is, when considered broadly, nationally, globally, as impersonal and resource-hungry as a car manufacturer or an industrial-scale food producer, you'll understand why, if you don't write stories about vampires, teen lovers or safely conventional middle-aged detectives, it is so fucking hard to get published.

Publishers want to publish good work, of course. They don't set out to publish shit. But more than wanting to publish good work, they want to publish work that sells.

And this means you have to decide what kind of writer you want to be. If you want to sell a shitload of copies, get flown around the world, bank six and seven-figure advances, then write the kind of stuff the big publishers want and be happy doing it and be happy spending the money.

But if you don't want to write that kind of stuff, if writing is more to you than just cobbling together a darn good tale, if you want to talk about things that aren't ordinarily talked about, say things that challenge the majority, that champion the minority, that call bullshit on all the bland, gutless hacks who make sure their wallets are firmly in their back pockets each time they sit down to write, then be that kind of writer. Be that kind of writer. Because somewhere in the world, at some point in time, your book will be needed. Not to wile away an hour or two before sleep, not to pass a holiday weekend lying on the beach, but to show someone, some other lonely, lost, hurting human being that they are not alone. And even if it is only one person, and even if that person lives on the other side of the planet, it is enough. It is enough when they turn the last page and set down your book, that they find their life forever changed because of what they have just read. Because of what you have written.

But if you are brave enough, or insane enough to write this way, don't expect a big advance and a contract with a major publisher. It might be safe not to expect even to earn a living. I'm not saying it can't happen—there are a handful of notable cases that prove it can—it's just that... it probably won't.

CREATIVELY MOURNING THE NOVEL

"The darker the night, the brighter the stars, the deeper the grief, the closer is God!"

—Fyodor Dostoevsky, *Crime and Punishment*

Heidegger's claim that we only form an identity after facing death has been stuck in my head since I first read about it at uni. We should remember this when considering the death of the novel.

I have always been interested in transformation, of art and of the personal identity. Life transforming into death. Death becoming something new entirely. I think if something isn't growing and developing then it will likely die like any other organism. It's a theme I've tried to explore in all my writing. In the main, I've written genre fiction with a philosophical edge, but recently I've been reading a lot of David Shields and Gore Vidal—now I'm thinking that the novel is a restricted, perishing medium in its current incarnation. In and of itself, the novel doesn't have the same power it used to, especially among this new distracted soma-generation of consumers: somnambulists in the perpetual quest of instant gratification. And, alarmingly, I think Neil Postman's doomsday hypothesis is coming true, in particular when he talks about humanity being simultaneously addicted to and oppressed by its own relentless search for amusement. But it's my belief that the written word can survive by latching on to other forms—art installation, music, cinema, etc. As writers, we are in the business of expanding the lifespan of literature. I wanted to create something for the ADHD consumer because ultimately it's this generation who will have the final say.

'Influence' started as a conversation between me and Edwin Sellors of Ragged Lion Press. Just a general chit-chat about the decline of independent literature. Edwin is a big proponent of the visual medium and has been making interesting (very literary) multimedia videos for his YouTube site for a long time. I had written these depressing little poems and they were just sitting around on my hard drive, so I decided to spruce them up a bit. I wrote this weird incidental music and recorded readings over the melody. On a whim, I sent them along to Edwin who immediately started splicing these public access images together to make a sort of hallucinogenic music video for the poems. I thought it looked cool—like he was teasing out this shadow archetype buried beneath my words, and we kept collaborating in this way. I'd send along a recording and Edwin would visualise it. Tease out the id.

I had just spent five years writing The DREGS Trilogy (which is a sprawling multi-stranded cosmic horror novel) and I felt artistically and spiritually exhausted by the process—and disheartened by the subsequent lack of attention the book earned. The amount of time spent thrashing out a layered novel felt disproportionate to the interest garnered. I've always written for the sake of writing because I was compelled to do it and I appreciate craft in any form, but I couldn't deny that something shifted. Please understand that the novel isn't dead to me, but it's perhaps in need of a tune-up somehow. If it's to grow.

Marcus du Sautoy argues that technology will allow new and important transformations to occur within books, and we are in the embryonic stages of this metamorphosis—I suppose this is my attempt to bring his theory into practice. And, by the way, I've been through the various anticipatory stages of the grieving process already. I've felt the initial shock and denial we all experienced when kindle came along; the anger and bargaining stage; depression. But now it's time for the upward turn. Reconstruction and working through the new world. 'Influence' is part of my acceptance and hope phase. We've mourned long enough and now it's time to do something about it.

Dennis Cooper does some really interesting things with his GIF novels, and I suppose 'Influence' is trying to capture something similar. A marriage of creative mediums to form a new incarnation of the novel. While the video-pieces themselves seem somewhat disparate, there is a common narrative thread throughout, and not a particularly oblique or abstract one. Simply put—'Influence' deals with all major forms of power: from the structured systemic exploitation of the government, to the individual corruption of the soul. The project could have just as easily been called 'Exploitation.' Dennis talks about composing his GIF novel, 'Zak's Haunted House,' according to the same principles, planning and structuring of a traditional novel. There is still skill involved, and a lot of the same skills we're used to as writers. Dennis presents the viewer/reader with stacked columns of images, a mood board that flashes and glitches. It's sensory in a way that traditional literature could never dream of being. And he's actually having fun with the novel (now who thought that was possible?). Earlier I talked about The DREGS Trilogy, and the exhaustion that its creation and subsequent release caused me—the truth is that I wouldn't have minded the lack of critical attention had the novels composition been a remotely enjoyable process.

Also, what stories are there left to tell? There's something to be said for Tumblr and internet art. This 'Dark Night of the Internet's Soul' is our new story written in HTML-code. If the internet and technology have killed the novel, or played a part in its demise, then these entities owe it to the art form to advance it somehow—and we owe the internet a place in the bookshelf of intellectual storytelling. We are in shadow times, and one thing we can do is utilise this predatory technology as a collaborator. I admit it's sort of sad to concede defeat like this, but if you can't beat them then maybe you should join them. In this instance anyway. You need to grow. To develop. Even as I write this I'm aware it's nothing ground-breaking—Duchamp's spinning roto-reliefs were creating hypnotic retinal illusions long before the contemporary transgressive came along.

'Influence' is a kind of bootleg item. There won't be many copies made, but there will be an album comprising all the spoken-word pieces, a chapbook of poetry, and a set of Philip LoPresti's B&W photography. It'll be a lovely item.

LIKE SOLZHENITSYN

Eight years in camps, now it wants in.
I won't let it.
It longs from the gutters,
writhes in the sumps,
even beneath the hood of my car.
I won't let it in.
Boils raise on my forearm, I burst them with a pin.
I still won't let it in.

But the city wants in so bad.
It's street lights hang, like a gang
of ominous petals on a black bough above the bazaar
and whang the skull uptown.

I can pretend that this place means something,
rip off the Band-Aid, show off my scar.
It really wants in.
I won't let it.

It crawls along the membrane, so thin.
I won't ever let it in, even as
my pores are clogged with city-stink,
eyeballs glued with grime and bathtub gin.
I still won't let it in, no, it's a prisoner
of my temple like Solzhenitsyn.
Submit to its hysteria and demands.
My identity is not this city.
It wants in.

HARD TO BEAT: WITH IAIN SINCLAIR

Who better to guide us through the abyss than a born adventurer? A man who would give Professor Challenger a run for his money. Lauded and derided in equal measure as flaneur, grand inquisitor, counter-cultural historian, compulsive chronicler and a pioneer of Situationist psychogeography, Iain Sinclair is candid regarding most aspects of his long-serving career (and always has been).

With his latest new book, *American Smoke*, he keeps his hallmark polychromatic prose, but dares to offer us something a little different this time around: a true homage to the great Beat generation. Like I mentioned before, the release of a new Sinclair book is usually a highly divisive affair: whether he's delving into Hackney's substrata, criticising the city's bleak artificial landscapes, comparing peasant poet John Clare to 'the elephant man' or offering his satirical readings of the Heathrow hinterlands, you can bet he'll be engendering controversy.

One thing is certain though, and that's that Iain Sinclair will be remembered long after his death as the country's ultimate post-punk diarist.

NOTE: The first thing to make clear is that this is not actually a conversation: except in the way that Nabokov regarded the interview, as something to be composed at his leisure, faked ventriloquism, the author often providing both questions and answers. I prefer to talk face to face, to digress, listen, before trying to arrive at a place we haven't visited before. So the form of the blog collision, with which I'm uneasy, is like a delayed-detonation playlet. A TV report from somewhere remote, with the interrogator waiting, painfully, for the question to register. And the interrogated standing dumb, in mid-shot, beside a road or a ruin, outside a secure building. The questions, in my case, sat on the desk for days, weeks: and then, a gap in the schedule appearing, they were dealt with at a rush, in a stuttering monologue.

Iain, you've lived in London for half a century now, what is it about the city that fascinates you so much?

Its unknowability. Its headbanging provocation. The way that every walk over the same ground is different. London started for me as the point of access to films I would never have tracked down on home ground. And now it's about keeping neural pathways open.

Of course, you're actually Welsh. Is national identity important to you? Has your homeland been as influential or inspiring as London when it comes to your writing? Are you ever compelled to write sprawling novels that explore human ecology and dystopian modernity in places like Cardiff or Swansea?

I'm suspicious of any form of nationalism. I grew up in Wales, but my father was of Scottish ancestry. He was gripped by the stories of his grandfather, a world-wanderer who wrote about his expedition to the headwaters of the Amazon in Peru. He was tasked with evaluating unknown (to London) territory on behalf of a coffee-planting company. My allegiance has always been to place, to certain long-remembered landscapes. I could never have attempted, without living there for years, a 'sprawling' novel about Cardiff or Swansea. But I was happy, thanks to the publishers Little Toller, to have been given the chance to return to Wales to write the monograph published as *Black Apples of Gower.*

Is it safe to say you're pretty unhappy with the contemporary London landscape and its architecture? I'm almost reluctant to bring up the Millennium Dome...

We're living now in what I take to be the 'last London.' A city so much estranged from its earlier identities (always shifting and revising) that it is unrecognizable. The process could be described as beginning with Margaret Thatcher and the manufacture of Canary Wharf and Docklands out of the Isle of Dogs. The Olympic Games (and other such grand events) were seen as the perfect smokescreen for enclosures, investment silos, improving the image of destruction. But I've talked myself out on these topics. The trick has been to find projects that pull away from those dead zones, and the promotional language of politicians and puffers, into ritual acts of exorcism. Walks, films, books. Downriver for Thatcher. London Orbital for the Dome and other millennial follies. Ghost Milk for Westfield and the Olympic piracy. London Overground for the doughnut of speculative railway suburbs, new-build blocks with artisan coffee and balconies for bikes.

In *American Smoke*, you actually leave London and relocate to the USA. Were American writers a big influence on you, the Beats especially?

My romantic side was drawn to the energies of Beat writing from way back. I was reading the Kerouac books as they appeared. And I was lucky enough, in my early twenties, to spend time filming with Allen Ginsberg at the time of the Dialectics of Liberation conference in 1967. It seemed to make sense, as a way of shaking free of the black-hole gravity of post-Olympic London, the corporate state, to reconnect with the myths of the Beat writers, as well as with pre-Beat outsider figures like Malcolm Lowry, and the post-Beat Chilean novelist and poet Roberto Bolaño. *American Smoke*, which I enjoyed writing very much, is about bad journeys, terminal quests, not getting to Mexico.

I read the book on the movie *Crash* you did for the BFI. I think it's safe to say that Ballard has been a significant influence on your work. Aside from appearing beside him briefly in the Mary Harron documentary and his contribution to "London: City of Disappearances," did you know Ballard well?

I got to know Ballard late on, around 1999, after hearing much about the seminal years of New Worlds and the fragmentary assembly of *The Atrocity Exhibition* from Michael Moorcock, a good friend. We used to have meals around Shepherds Bush, every few months, with Ballard and his 'girlfriend,' Claire Walsh. So I became familiar with social aspects of the man, but I wouldn't say that I got to know him any better as time went on. He was always engaging. He never talked about his work or the books he was involved with. He might call for a special bottle to celebrate the end of some project and the start of the next one. Beyond anything else, he remained the professional writer. He wasn't as alien and forbidding a presence as William Burroughs, but the central mystery was always a mystery.

I heard you have a few Burroughs first editions on your bookshelf too. You corresponded briefly with Burroughs via airmail. Can you tell us about what kind of relationship you both had?

I didn't know Burroughs at all. Even though I met him a couple of times and spent one long afternoon with him in Lawrence, Kansas. He was an earlier and more viral influence than Ballard. As I got to know Jim, I appreciated what he was doing more and more. The coolness, the clarity. The heroic and undeceived perversity. Burroughs wasn't perverse, strangely enough. He was a prose-poet with a formidable sense of otherness. You had to know him much better than I did to excavate the humanity and the bite of the humour. I corresponded with him as a student and published one of his pieces in Dublin. Then we tried to set up a film for West German television, but he decided, at that moment, to get immersed in Scientology.

Can you tell us a little about Psychogeography?

I don't think there is any more than can be said. The topic has outlived its usefulness and become a brand.

Do you see similar parallels between yourself and Kerouac? Do you think *On the Road* could be considered one of the original staples in the field of psychogeography?

On the Road, even after the editors 'normalised' certain aspects of how the work is presented, is about raw excitement, long-breath, open-field composition; neurotic rhythms, risk, astonishing sensory memory and fluid juxtaposition of detail. It's not a Situationist work or a strategic, confrontational piece. It's ripe with premature nostalgia and celebration of territory, shamanic restlessness.

Do you think you'll return to poetry or the graphic novel format in *Slow Chocolate Autopsy*? I really loved that book.

I never left poetry, as such. It's just that the way I published became more and more covert. I preferred to operate on my own terms, through micro-presses (including my own). I have a new gathering called *Seeschlange* coming along from Rod Mengham's Equipage. Etruscan Books, run by the ever-engaging Nicholas Johnson, published a substantial selection of the poetry I produced after *Suicide Bridge*, as *The Firewall*, with a generous introductory note from Michael McClure. But I'm not sure that anybody noticed. Skylight, a press based in Cheltenham, did a new edition of *Lud Heat* and a revised and extended edition of *Suicide Bridge* (the version I'm happiest with, even though they sold about six copies). I don't see a way, at the moment, to get back to the stories and graphic strips of that collaboration with Dave McKean, *Slow Chocolate Autopsy*. There are new and uncollected Norton stories. And Norton has been promoted into making cameo appearances in Alan Moore's *The League of Extraordinary Gentlemen*. If there was any publishing interest—unlikely—I'd be delighted to make a return to this form.

You have your own distribution label. Do you have any thoughts or opinions on the current state of the publishing industry in general?

With mainstream publishing ever more corporate and short-termist, it's a good time for the independents. Great things are still being produced, but nobody makes any money. Which gives it all a certain survivalist edge. And relish.

My magazine, Imperial Youth Review, featured a comic strip by Steve Aylett that originally featured in Alan Moore's *Dodgem Logic*. How did you and Alan Moore come to be associated with one another?

I met Alan around the time of *From Hell*. He was interested in, and generous about, the weirdness of *Lud Heat*, with its arcane speculations and the conspiratorial aspects of *White Chappell, Scarlet Tracings*. We were involved in a number of subversive London performances. Then I came to Northampton to read with Brian Catling, an evening that ended with a gunman among the graves, and an episode Alan draws on in *Voice of the Fire*. Alan was part of the recent English Journey tour. And he did nice turns in the two Andrew Kötting films, *Swandown* and *By Our Selves*. I've just finished reading Alan's remarkable local epic, *Jerusalem*. It will take five years to absorb it fully.

I am a profoundly unhappy person and my job reflects and compliments my misery. What's the worst job you've ever had?

I've never had a *real* job: parks gardener, white-lines-on-Hackney-Marshes, ullage cellar in a brewery, loading and unloading containers in old Stratford—that wasn't frustrating or infuriating at certain times. But, in essence, I enjoyed them all. For themselves. For what they told me about London, and my fellow workers. And as future material for written and unwritten books. The worst days were probably handling toxic materials or dripping sheep casings in Chobham Farm in the bitterest deeps of winter. But, as ever, the worse it got, the better the potential routines. All life is a paragraph waiting to be shaped and exploited.

CURATING HORROR: ELLEN DATLOW

After over thirty-five years in the editing game, there aren't many people out there more respected or critically acclaimed than Ellen Datlow. In a long, prestigious career (that's seen her win seven Hugo's, ten World Fantasy Awards, two British Fantasy Awards, five Bram Stokers, three Shirley Jacksons, and twelve Locus Awards) Datlow has cemented herself as something of an institution in the field of science fiction, fantasy, and horror. Our very own arbiter for great writing and truly terrifying tales.

With over ninety anthologies to her name, the New York native is considered by many to be the leading authority on which authors we should all be reading within those genres—and, while she has never looked twice at a story I've written or been involved with, it's difficult to dispute this claim.

Ellen, you always hear people asking authors which other writers inspired them, but do you have any editorial influences? Anyone's approach or style that you really admired or motivated you to head down a similar path so enthusiastically?

Judith Merril, Maxwell Perkins, and Harlan Ellison. Merril for her Bests of the Year, which included fiction from all types of magazines and reprinted stories by Bernard Malamud, Isaac Bashevis Singer, Romain Gary, Muriel Spark, Bertrand Russell, Jules Feiffer, John D. McDonald, and many other writers not known for their SF, paving the way for the blurring of genre boundaries. Maxwell Perkins for his dedication and encouragement to some of the United States' greatest novelists. Harlan Ellison for pushing writers into then-taboo territory with *Dangerous Visions* and *Again, Dangerous Visions*.

Your eighth *Best Horror of the Year* volume was recently published, and I was wondering—what's the screening process like for a project of that magnitude? I mean, you must receive thousands of entries from eager candidates, myself included. Do people send you stories or do you actively seek them out?

I don't solicit "entries." I solicit *publishers* to send me their magazines/files of stories from websites, entire anthologies and collections. The only reason I should be sent an individual submission is if I can't get the material through the publisher. Contributors should be pushing their publishers to send me and every other year's best editor their books/stories. I rarely read self-published work, unless it's by someone already established by having first published traditionally.

***Nightmares, a New Decade of Modern Horror*, a companion anthology to *Darkness: Two Decades of Modern Horror*, recently hit the shelves—I'm curious about your experience**

compiling that book. Do you encounter a lot of hurdles in the editing process? Has there ever been any backlash from a writer you turned down or refused to work with?'

I was eager to edit an anthology of newer stories as soon as *Darkness* was published in 2010. But Tachyon, my publishers, convinced me to wait until I could cover the next ten years: 2005-2015. No obstacles—it's just difficult to pick the best of the best, which essentially is what the two volumes represent in my mind.

Sometimes, when editing a best of the year, I can't acquire the rights to a story I'd like to use, for one reason or another. That always bothers me because it means that this one, terrific story that I love, won't be shared with my readers (of course, they might have read the story wherever it was originally published).

When editing an original anthology, sometimes writers on whom I've been counting don't come through with their story. Or the story doesn't work for the anthology, and I've got to turn it down. This is the reason that I and many other editors of original anthologies ask about one third more writers than we actually need for any given anthology. We know that about one third will drop out.

Back in my OMNI Magazine days, I received a few nasty rants by rejected writers, all of whom swore they'd never send me another story. They did, all of them within about three years. And not one ever acknowledged his assholery nor apologized.

The anthology, *Children of Lovecraft*, came out this year too. How has the book performed commercially and has the reception been what you expected—I know it was released by Dark Horse who are seen primarily as a publisher of graphic novels?

This is my third Lovecraftian anthology (the reprint anthology *Lovecraft's Monsters* was published in 2014 by Tachyon) and my second for Dark Horse—the first was *Lovecraft Unbound*, back in 2009 (*Children of Lovecraft* is my fourth anthology for Dark Horse). They've published single-author collections and several novels in the past, and so far, have been supportive of the anthologies of mine that they've published.

I don't know how the book is doing commercially—I won't know for quite a while, but generally, Lovecraftian anthologies and novels continue to sell and sell, which is why my editor asked me to edit this second one for them.

Also, I'm sure you're asked this a lot, but what are your thoughts on HP Lovecraft himself? He's come under some heavy criticism from certain corners of the horror community for his personal ideologies; do you think it's easy to separate the art from the artist?

Lovecraft was a racist and anti-Semite. There's no arguing against that. And his work's influence on weird/dark fiction and weird/dark fiction writers is also unassailable. I've recently responded to a question from another interviewer essentially explaining that

I read Lovecraft when I was very young and was not cognizant (nor interested in) metaphor or symbolism in fiction. And I knew nothing about Lovecraft the person—was unaware of the scholarship on him or his correspondence or his poetry. Basically, all I knew were the stories and novels set in his mythos. I appreciated the cosmic horror he depicted. In a way, it's poetic justice that so many writers—of all sexes, races, and ethnicities—are using his works as a playground to create new stories and new themes, rather than submissively imitate them as so many of his "circle" did, way back when.

People see you as something of a gatekeeper in the field of horror and science fiction, do you ever feel the pressure of that responsibility? Does this provide a driving force when compiling an anthology, knowing you have a certain weight of audience expectation on your shoulders?

Every editor is a gatekeeper. That's a large portion of any acquisition editor's job: to make choices. To decide what goes into a magazine, a webzine, an anthology—and what doesn't. There are plenty of other short story editors and markets out in the world, so if one editor turns down a story, the writer just needs to send it to another one.

I'm a reader first and foremost. I'm a reader who loves short stories and loves working with writers on their work to help them make it better. I'm lucky that most of my anthologies sell well enough that I can continue to edit new ones. I please my readers by pleasing myself, which is why I'll only work on a theme that I believe will generate really interesting stories.

What advice would you give a writer who maybe wants to feature in one of your anthologies? Is there a style that appeals to you or that you find repellent?

First of all, I don't read unsolicited manuscripts. If a writer is published in a venue I check out while reading for the *Best Horror of the Year* (and that's most magazines/anthologies that publish sf/f/h and even crime/mysteries) I'll likely start noticing their work and one day I might solicit a story from them for something else.

What I buy depends on what anthology theme I'm working on. When I solicit stories, I send out guidelines to the writers in whom I'm interested. In those guidelines, I usually give an idea of what I do and don't want. And as I start to acquire stories for that anthology and it fills up, I'll contact the writers who have promised me stories to let them know that I don't want to see any more...such and such type of story.

It's difficult for young writers in a market that's become so over-saturated—do you have any tips for people who want desperately to stand out from the crowd?

Write your heart out and submit to markets that have a high profile. Don't give your work away because very few "for love" markets have any distribution. Keep writing, keep submitting work. If you seek feedback, first make sure you trust whoever is giving it to you. Don't send out first drafts. Once you finish a story, let it sit for a little while (not too long). Reread it. Revise if you feel it needs it. Then send it out. Do not wait for a response. Write your next story. Rinse and repeat.

THE LESSONS OF DIARMUID HESTER'S 'WRONG'

We come to life in a cold open. We get no initial preparation before the freight-train of self-awareness comes hurtling by to drag our newfound consciousness through the common quagmires of loneliness, criticality, and overwhelming emotional turmoil. It can take us a long time to work out our own motivations, never mind those of the other sentient body sitting across from us. Diarmuid Hester's critical biography of Dennis Cooper made me realise something I've been wrestling with for over a decade—why do books like *Frisk*, *Closer* and *The Sluts* appeal to me so much? I've always wondered what the appeal was (beyond great writing)—and as a straight man from the West of Scotland it might not be immediately clear why these specific narratives resonate with me in such a wholly profound way. Things feel a little clearer after reading *Wrong*.

I realise that Dennis Cooper is on a similar quest for safe fraternity. Another soul aimlessly pawing through the social-night for a stray lantern of genuine friendship and finding mostly teeth and automata. And it's this doomed pursuit of reciprocity that resonates.

Hester does a masterful job of merging academic analysis with succinct biographical detail. He is an accomplished writer in his own right who we should be hearing more from in the very near future. And he starts at the beginning, detailing Coopers affluent but fractured family theatre of alcoholism, tragedy and even DC's own dark thoughts linked with lust and violence throughout early childhood. It's funny, DC never discusses any of these topics with shame or unease. He understands them completely, pragmatically. Finding artistic kinship in DeSade and Rimbaud, we find a man who has gone searching for his tribe early on. Yet he still gets burned.

Hester's book also gives us a crucial insight into the central figure of George Miles, the preoccupation of DC's career-long thesis. *Wrong* charts Miles' tragic death in 1987 and the development from burgeoning friendship to romantic dependant. This focal point is where all these ideas of fraternity and loneliness come together. George Miles becomes a Bressonian mannequin through which Cooper can communicate important and rarely-discussed universal facts. That true friendship is rare and complicated.

Cooper's characters are always moving monochromatically—vacant, distracted, detached or in philosophical meditation with their own individuality. He frequently explores a common intrasubjectve masculine fantasy that eludes many of us—connection with other people. And connection is something DC's characters can rarely achieve, except through sex and violence. Cooper gives us a blank slate while consciously dismantling the binary logic of narrativity. This is an extraordinary gift. Like therapy.

Wrong also shows us the countless attempts at connection Cooper has made throughout his life—from his relationship with

Amy Gerstler, to embracing the New York Romantic aesthetic and even a stint on college radio. I'm reminded of another fantastic book that came out this year in Thomas Moore's *Alone*. It is impossible to chronicle any journey into adulthood or loss of innocence without probing violence. Violence is, after all, a contact sport—flesh on flesh. It comes at us suddenly during the cold open, before eventually destroying the corporeal form and distorting into something unique. If you let it. Like Rimbaud, Cooper and Moore are desperate to grab, articulate and preserve that lost seed of bygone youth when friendship and connection seemed a simpler more achievable deed. Where once it could be defined by a simple school seating chart or a love of morning cartoons, as adult men, connection becomes an intensely challenging feat.

It is the desire of most cognisant beings to achieve meaningful connection, yet many of us settle in secret sadness for surface-level interactions. Why do we do this? Reading Dennis Cooper will help you through this depressing reality. Art as experience is destined to be filtered through the mediated process of subjectivity. It is posited by Hester that these Bressonian mannequins (also see DC's work of Gisele Vienne) are a deliberate extension of Cooper's distancing aesthetic, allowing the reader to project their own traits, like a first-person video game. But I would actually argue that the inner lives are articulated well. These distant, jaded boys are exhausted and 'deep.' We just never 'know' it. As no one could ever 'know' it. The harsh reality that we can never really 'know' anyone. Another depressing reality.

There is an interesting study of the mathematical approach to the Cycle, again highlighting the supposed robotic surface methodology of probing the adolescent idol. But one thing is clear: Cooper has been concerned with the individual and community building from the beginning of his career. He knows what he's talking about. By honing an aesthetic of distance in his work, Cooper expresses the great battle between man's universal goal of solitude and his desire for community. He hopes that we might seek union through mental and physical exploration after accepting the depressing realities of our mental and physical distance. People argue that Cooper's books are amoral, but they explore ideas of connection with such fervour—and are honest in the portrayal of its failure.

Cooper eventually finds his modern community, his tribe, via his blog (something he can control and interface with on his own terms). DC has suffered some intense betrayals—JT Leroy (aka, 'Terminator'), the rise and heartbreak of Little Caesar Press, and his general disenchantment with New York—but he is a man who does not give up on people. Ever. He teaches us, and actively encourages us, to keep believing in the goodness and potential of people—while forcing us to look at the harsh reality of its intrinsic complexity. He is the ultimate rarity in any lit circle—an established writer who is a natural caregiver. So, let's not let him down. He's doing all of this for us. Scrapbooking us all into obscurity. Together in the only real way he knows how. This is our collective marbled swarm.

Addendum: Conversation with Diarmuid Hester

Diarmuid, what kind of kid were you growing up and how did you first come into contact with the work of Dennis Cooper?

I was a sad kid, kind of haughty, very particular. Pretty lonely too—at least until I joined a band at 16. I remember we did Irish-language versions of rock tracks. 'Killing in the Name Of' was 'Ag Marú in Ainm'. There was something perverse about translating vibrant, angry (mostly American) sentiments into a language that felt so dry and dead to me at the time. I've always loved the idiosyncratic approach.

I came across Dennis' work first in 2006 when I was doing a masters in queer studies. We read *Frisk*, and were encouraged to think about Dennis' outsider status vis-a-vis queer subculture. My classmates hated the book, but I thought it was incredible. I went on to write my PhD about him. As I said, I've got a lot of time for an idiosyncratic approach.

Did you have any early/memorable experiences of existential crisis?

I had one big crisis. This would've been in my mid-20s. I'd finished a masters in philosophy, and had about six months of absolute despair. Couldn't find meaning in anything. Everything, all systems of valuation, interpretation, significance were artificial, cobbled-together, unnatural. Thus worthless. Looking back, I was exhausted and depressed, but my feelings were also interwoven with an intellectual commitment to nihilism. You see, during the masters I'd worked with Ray Brassier, the brilliant Glaswegian philosopher of nihilism, on a dissertation about Pierre Guyotat. It was basically a nihilist-inflected reading of Guyotat. That experience allowed me to develop this really rigorous nihilistic worldview, which was impossible to shake. I still haven't shaken it off—and to be honest I wouldn't want to. Yes, human life is without inherent meaning or purpose. Yes, meaning-making systems like culture are improvised and ultimately baseless. But isn't that what makes existence fascinating (and also faintly absurd)?

How do you feel about fraternity? Do you have a sense of community or a desire to be part of a broader social group?

Community, at least *intentional* community, the community we create rather than the one we're born into and inherit, is really important to me. If I tell you I've been a queer Irish immigrant for most of the past twenty years, you'll probably understand why. That's the reason I was so interested in the community that formed around Dennis' blog. Why in *Wrong* I wanted to describe it and preserve an impression of it for posterity.

Do you think independent writers owe a great debt to artists like Dennis Cooper?

Dennis' impact is huge. Obviously his style and literary aesthetic, which are so unique and so absolutely unprecedented, have had an enormous influence on contemporary writing, and the approach taken by many indie writers. But he's been so influential in other, less visible ways too: he's helped to create communities for writers to support each other and learn from each other (e.g. in LA or on his blog); his editorial work made opportunities for a host of unknown writers (e.g. the Little House on the Bowery series for Akashic Books); he's always ready with a blurb or a word of praise for indie writers he likes, who may be completely unknown to others, to help them to gain wider recognition.

Your background is firmly rooted in academia, but do you think you'll ever branch out to fiction?

I don't know about firmly rooted, but yes I've been an academic for a while. I get tired of some scholarly conversations though—where privileged educated people talk to other privileged educated people in a language only they understand in subscription-only journals. I've no interest in that kind of academia. My recent work is more cultural history, non-fiction, written for a broad readership. My new book is coming out with a trade publisher, which I'm very happy about. I'm excited about that form of writing right now, and I've no plans to move away from it any time soon.

A VERY AMBITIOUS MAGICIAN: DENNIS COOPER

Dennis, it's really great to speak with you. I was devastated to have missed your recent mini Scottish tour—I hear from friends that the Q&A at Glasgow University was a tremendous success. I hope you come back to Scotland sometime in the near future.

Hi, Chris, thanks. The Glasgow screening was great. Zac and I were very happy. And, of course, I too hope I can back to Scotland soon.

Your latest foray into cinema, *Permanent Green Light*, provides such a singular construal of detachment and nihilism—but were there any filmmakers or artists who inspired your particular vision or who motivated you stylistically? It really does stand apart from most of the things I've watched in 2019.

It's probably not unusual for a filmmaker to say this, but Zac and I were truly trying to make a film that was unique and our own. We didn't have any role models in mind. Robert Bresson is my favorite artist, and I'm sure his influence is in this film, although the numerous comparisons of our film to Bresson's films really overdo the relationship there. It's common for a new artist's work—and, even though I've been making other kinds of work for forever, film is new to both Zac and me—to immediately be cross-referenced to the works of known artists. It's a strange habit people have of looking for something already familiar in the new rather than exploring what's unfamiliar about it.

When I was first publishing books, critics were always saying I was the new Burroughs or Genet or whatever, until they finally figured out what I was doing and let my work name itself. So, there are no guiding light films or filmmakers for our film, or not consciously at least. I would imagine there are impactful traces in the film from filmmakers that Zac and I both particularly like a lot: Bresson, James Benning, Chantal Akerman, Straub/Huillet, Terrence Malick, and others.

Your George Miles Cycle is often described as a semi-autobiographical work. I was wondering, are there any emotional or psychological echoes between you and any of the characters in *Permanent Green Light*? The film seems quick to denounce any cultural connections to terrorism (or any notion of ideological purpose)—instead, there's a rather romantic view of teenage angst, and suicide in particular (in the sense that it's played very clinically, honestly, and without analysis)—would

you say you've ever been obsessed with suicide or death? Were you a morbid adolescent? I suppose we'd all love to go out with a memorable explosion.

No, not that I know of. Zac and I don't really think of the characters as real people equivalents. They're just the most present and influential elements of the film at large to us. So, no, the film isn't autobiographical. I also don't think it's true the film is romantic about teenage angst and suicide at all. I think the film takes the characters' ideas and feelings and actions very seriously, and that's a very different thing.

I've written about suicide and death very frequently since I started being an artist. I don't think I was morbid when I was young. I wasn't suicidal or anything like that. I just wanted to understand things that were very confusing and powerful to me. There was a fair amount of suicide around me. My great friend George Miles tried to commit suicide twice as a teen and did finally kill himself. My uncle blew his brains out. A close friend of my family killed himself in our house. So that was there, and that surely influenced my fascination with writing about suicide as a way to figure out the reasoning behind it and its heavy impact.

Roman, the main character in *Permanent Green Light*, doesn't intentionally commit suicide. That's not his interest or goal. Others around him do, and he studies those suicides for his project. He wants instead to disappear in a way that has the most spectacular effect on the world that's possible. He decides that his death is the way to achieve maximum impact, and his goal is to die without triggering any conventional, personal reaction to death, and to his death in particular. He's trying to create a death/disappearance that erases him entirely and just uses the natural, inherent impact that suicide has as a powerful effect. He doesn't long to die. He's more like a very ambitious magician, I think.

How did you and co-director Zac Farley first cross paths and when did you decide to collaborate?

Zac and I met about seven years ago. We just felt an immediate affinity and connection, and we started collaborating on projects very soon after we met. The opportunity arose for us to make our first film, *Like Cattle Towards Glow*, because I had written a script years before that no one was interested in producing, and, years later, after I'd met Zac, a German producer heard about the script and wanted to make it, which we did for extremely little money as a kind of experiment. So filmmaking just kind of fell into our laps. Zac is a visual artist and had made video works, but never a film, and I'd never been involved in making a film before. We loved making the film, and it got a very good response, so we fell in love with filmmaking, and now we hope to continue making films together.

The indie film landscape is looking pretty healthy right now (to an outsider like me), but was the pre/post-production or filmmaking process a complicated one? Was it easy to get *Permanent Green Light* produced and distributed? It seems like a tough elevator pitch.

I would say the indie filmmaking landscape is a very mixed bag at the moment. If you want to make a stylish but conventional indie film, especially if it fits into a popular genre or addresses trending social issues in a very fore-fronted way, it's a good time. If you want to make films that are adventurous and try to do something deeply new and fresh and original, that doesn't look or sound like a standard narrative indie film, it's actually a rough time. The indie film scene is quite conservative these days, I think. Most of the films that critics and people go ape for and consider adventurous tend to just play the game with a bit of a personal stamp on them. In most cases, if you don't have an at least a minor "name" actor in a main role, or use a score by a buzzy rock member or composer, or use a lot of artsy color saturation in your visuals or make a film that costs or looks like it cost at least a million dollars, you have a hard time getting films made, and then an even harder time getting them programmed in film festivals, much less released in theatres. On the other hand, there is a growing scene around experimental film right now. There are a lot of very interesting and daring young filmmakers making films for little money, and there's an increasing support system for showing and publicizing that work—venues, magazines, festivals, and so on. But it's an entirely separate scene from the standard film festival circuit and media coverage for indie film. That's very exciting and promising.

It wasn't hard to get *Permanent Green Light* produced. The head of a French production company, Local Films, saw and really liked *Like Cattle Towards Glow*, and he gave us the opportunity. And the budget for our film was pretty low, so we were able to raise the money through government grants here in France and a foundation in the US. It hasn't been an easy film to distribute for the reasons I mentioned above. It doesn't fit in, which is the film's strength, I think, but distributors and festival programmers, while always saying how much they liked the film, didn't know what to do with it because it doesn't have a pre-set marketable tag, and that's what they want. It got distributed in France, and it had a tiny theatre release in the US where it's on some good streaming platforms. But that, and continuing screenings around the world, are it so far. Zac and I think very long term about these things, and we feel confident the film will have a long life with increasing visibility and acknowledgment. So, given the tough situation, we're actually very happy with how it has gone for the film. The response to the film from people who've seen it has been really fantastic.

I know Todd Verow adapted *Frisk* into a sort of cold-porn drama in 1995, but would you like to see any of your other books translated onto the silver screen? There is something inherently 'literary' about your work.

That awful *Frisk* experience soured me on letting my novels be adapted for film. I've been extremely cautious ever since. Honestly, I'm not interested in my books being filmed, and I'm pretty happy that almost all of them would be impossible to adapt. They're very much literature and books. They're all about what language can do and the relationship between written text and the imagination of a person reading them one-on-one in complete privacy and what can happen as a consequence. They're finished. They're not interim things waiting for a different kind of representation. So, yeah, the film adaptation idea isn't something I'm interested in. But if a filmmaker wanted to adapt one of my works and had a very interesting reason for wanting to, and had thought carefully about what would happen if the work became visuals rather than words on pages, I would definitely be interested in talking with him or her or them about the possibility.

You're a big fan of world cinema. You relocated to Paris, why did you decide to move there and, ultimately, to make a movie in France?

Well, living in Paris was a lifelong dream of mine. I've been a Francophile practically since I was born. Technically, I moved here because my boyfriend was Russian, and he couldn't get a visa to enter the US, but he could travel to France easily. So I came here to be with him. My books were published and known here, and that made the move seem easier. Also, I had just started collaborating with the French theatre director/choreographer Gisele Vienne, whose works I've been writing since 2004, and living here allowed us to work together closely. So that was an impetus too. As far as making films here, that just happened because I live here and Zac is French and lives in Paris too. Also, it's much easier to get funding for films here than in the US. Much, much easier. I love Paris. Moving here is definitely one of the best things that's ever happened to me.

Music plays such a huge part in your work. Do you foresee working on any projects within that medium? I'd love to see you team up with Guided by Voices to produce a concept album.

Collaborating with Guided by Voices is a mega-dream idea, but the big problem is that Robert Pollard is a genius lyric writer, so there would be literally nothing for me to do in the collaboration. I love the idea of collaborating with musicians. Stephen O'Malley of the band Sunn O))) writes the music for Gisele's pieces, so I get to collaborate with them through her. The electronic music artist Puce Mary, whose work I love, is doing the sound/score for Zac's and my next film, so we'll be working with her in a close and intricate way, which is exciting. But, yeah, I'm totally game to collaborate with bands and musicians. If the opportunity arose, and if it made sense, I would jump at that.

ACKNOWLEDGEMENTS

"Demonstration" originally appeared in *SELFFUCK*

"I Transgress" originally appeared on *Dennis Cooper's Blog*

"Combat Shock: Buddy Giovinazzo" originally appeared at *Bizarro Central*

"Blood Eagle" originally appeared in *SELFFUCK*

"Oikeiôsis, Getting the Band Together: with Steve Finbow" originally appeared in *3:AM Magazine*

"Visiting Hours" originally appeared at *The Scottish Poetry Library*

"Pointlessly Devoted" originally appeared in *3:AM Magazine*

"Tidal River" originally appeared in *Lovecraft eZine*

"The Anti-Pornographer: From Danny Wylde to Chris Zeischegg" originally appeared in *SELFFUCK*

"Crimes of Indifference and the Barbarism of Love" originally appeared in *The Airgonaut*

"Creatively Mourning the Death of the Novel" originally appeared in *Invert/Extant*

"Like Solzhenitsyn" originally appeared in *3:AM Magazine*

"Hard to Beat: Iain Sinclair" originally appeared in *Sensitive Skin*

"Curating Horror: Ellen Datlow" originally appeared in *Dark Discoveries*

"The Lessons of Diarmuid Hester's, 'Wrong,'" originally appeared in *Invert/Extant*

"A Very Ambitious Magician: Dennis Cooper" originally appeared in *3:AM Magazine*

ABOUT THE AUTHOR

Chris Kelso is a multi-translated bestselling author and editor from Scotland. His short fiction has been nominated for a British Fantasy Award, and he is the two-time winner of Novel of the year from Ginger Nuts of Horror (2016/17). You can find his work in 3:AM, Sensitive Skin, Invert/Extant, The Scottish Poetry Library, Locus, Black Static and many more.

www.ingramcontent.com/pod-product-compliance
Lightning Source LLC
Chambersburg PA
CBHW030931060726
47591CB00005B/1754

* 9 7 8 1 9 5 4 8 9 9 0 1 8 *